IS MANAGER'S GUIDE TO
Implementing
and Managing
Internet
Technology

IS MANAGER'S GUIDE TO

Implementing
and Managing
Internet
Technology

2001 Supplement

RICHARD BARRETT CLEMENTS

PRENTICE HALL

This publication is designed to provide accurate and authoritative information in regard to the subject matter covered. It is sold with the understanding that the publisher is not engaged in rendering legal, accounting, or other professional service. If legal advice or other expert assistance is required, the services of a competent professional person should be sought.

—From a Declaration of Principles jointly adopted by a Committee of the American Bar Association and a Committee of Publishers and Associations.

Printed in the United States of America

10   9   8   7   6   5   4   3   2   1

ISBN 0-13-030674-6

ATTENTION: CORPORATIONS AND SCHOOLS

Prentice Hall books are available at quantity discounts with bulk purchase for educational, business, or sales promotional use. For information, please write to: Prentice Hall Direct Special Sales, 240 Frisch Court, Paramus, NJ 07652. Please supply: title of book, ISBN, quantity, how the book will be used, date needed.

PRENTICE HALL
Paramus, NJ 07652

On the World Wide Web at http://www.phdirect.com

Preface

The internet literally travels at the speed of light. New innovations and technologies are constantly being developed. These form ripples and patterns. Some collect together to form waves that stir up revolutions on the internet and in the real world.

Two of these revolutions dominate the internet technologies for the year 2001. The first is the massive rise in e-commerce. Nearly every company is moving towards using the internet as a medium for trade of products and services. Thousands of new companies are also forming on the internet every week to sell items. Services like eBay have attacked the retail price structure of the entire world. Any competent IS manager had better be aware of what e-commerce represents and know how to take his or her company into this new world.

The second revolution is broadband availability. When the original *IS Manager's Guide to Implementing and Managing Internet Technology* was written, the majority of people connected to the internet via modem at speeds up to 56kbs. Today, individuals and companies can connect at T1 speeds of 1.5 Megs per second using cable modems, wireless networks, or DSL phone lines. The cost of these access speeds have dropped dramatically in just one year. This new level of service access to the internet makes possible a wide variety of services. For example, you can truly teleconference with 30 frame per second video and CD quality sound. You can watch your favorite movie at any time. Your training department can have a worldwide audience. Again, the IS manager has to be in a position to seize these changes and profit their company or organization.

This supplement is dedicated to that task. We will look at the new technologies coming to market and how to harness the growing trends. At the same time, we will stay interactive by providing you with access to our web site (www.9000.net) and our e-mail address (clements@voyager.net). We will keep you up to date on developments.

How This Supplement Will Help You

In the original *IS Manager's Guide to Implementing and Managing Internet Technology,* we introduced several ideas, such as planning, project management, proper use of procedures, and the like to help you manage your internet presence. Many of these ideas are valid no matter what new developments occur on the internet.

However, the internet is history's greatest spawning ground for new ideas, concepts, and technologies. A few of these will impact your company and the way you manage your internet presence. Take the example of digital subscriber lines (DSL). This service wasn't available when we wrote the original book just over a year ago. Yet it is going to have a massive impact on the internet. The T1 speed of DSL is available for less than $200, versus the $1,200 price of a T1 line.

Such cost reductions and newer technologies will force you to completely reconsider your internet strategy at least once a year. Therefore, these supplements are designed to help you keep up with what has changed. In this first supplement, we are addressing e-commerce, broadband options, and the changing relationship between you and your internet provider.

We will provide you with guidelines and insights you can use to keep on top of these developments. Most of the content of this supplement is the result of feedback we have received from the readers of the original book. In addition, we had a good response to the supporting web site for this book:

www.9000.net

And you can reach the primary author at clements@voyager.net. We like to hear from you and answer your questions. In this way we can alert you to important changes as they happen.

Those of you that followed our monthly progress on the web site know that I finally put a bullet through our Windows NT server we used to test the concepts in the original book. By repeatedly crashing and abusing that machine, we have learned a lot about how to properly run internet technology within an organization. The Linux machine we set up is still purring away in a corner serving up web pages on an intranet and to the internet. The computer is a salvaged Pentium 120 with Linux and Apache (both free software). Experiments like this help us to see where the future of internet technology is headed.

Contents

Chapter S2
Building an e-Commerce Site   37

Chapter S3

The Broadband Revolution 77

Chapter S4
Security Revisited   105

Chapter S5

Keeping the Job You Have or Creating the Job You Want

Chapter S6

Implementing Wireless, Bots, and Other New Technologies

Appendix A

How to Find and Retain Good IS People   159

Appendix B

Implementing an Internet Project   165

Appendix C

Keeping Up with Your Newfound Internet Responsibilities   171

Index   179

Chapter S1
The e-Commerce Revolution

By now someone in your company is talking about e-commerce. Defined broadly, e-commerce is the process of conducting commerce through the internet. This can be anything from auction sites to web-based catalogs to internet ordering to software distribution to customers over the internet to electronic payment systems. In this chapter, we are going to look at how to perform sales over the internet. In the next chapter we will review how you set up and manage e-commerce sites.

It may seem a little odd to start by discussing sales tactics first. However, as we state in the original book, IS people tend to be seduced by hardware and software. As we shall see, it is far better to start by forming a sales strategy, develop marketing objectives, and then worry about how to execute your plans. Choice of software and hardware comes just about last in the process.

Selling on the Internet

The internet is a wild place. This is the conclusion of a special study team set up in May of 1998 to look into the effectiveness of selling on the internet. The team was set up by Solution Specialists (Grand Rapids, Michigan), a management consulting company that also engages in think-tank activities. At that time, Solution Specialists had several client companies that were selling products and services on the internet. In fact, Solution Specialists itself had sold many services on the Internet.

It was noted by a leading manager that the promise of the internet was not being fulfilled. That is, the large potential market of the internet should have resulted in a dramatic amount of new accounts and sales. This was not the case, and a team was formed to look into the matter. Specifically, how were people selling on the internet and was it effective?

This team was given a free hand to explore and experiment. In their initial meetings, all agreed that the internet was a fast growing market that would soon be the biggest sales territory in the world. However, something was missing. Where were the Coke/Pepsi types of competitions for advertising and marketing? Where were the large corporate sales staffs working the internet?

The analogy the group established was that the internet was like North America at the point of European discovery. There were trading posts everywhere but no organized system of trade. Any small, well-organized army could overrun the territory. It was this military analogy that would dominate the thinking of this study group.

The first step was to carefully define the nature of the internet and the customers located there.

1. *The internet is not like other markets.*

   The conventional sales model used on the internet at the time of this study was the "storefront" or "shopping mall" model. Essentially, you established an on-line store using a web page to present goods or services for sale. It was supposed to be like a giant shopping mall where a single internet user could select to shop at any store.

   As the failure of shopping mall sites on the internet can demonstrate, this model had problems. The study team identified several flaws in its logic. For example, there are over three million "stores" on the internet, each only a click away. It is like a shopping mall with three million stores and every store is just one foot step away from all the others. Thus, a single store will have great difficulty in being found, and customers can be whisked away in a single mouse click.

   The internet also has no dimensions in time or space. A traditional sales territory can be described in terms of a specific area. Traditional market segments can be defined by age and buying habits or lifestyles. With the ability to move around the world in an instant and have nearly complete anonymity, the traditional descriptions of market targets do not work.

Instead, you need to find where your potential customers linger on the internet. These are now called "internet communities." Places like CNN, eBay, and Yahoo are all examples of "communities." These are the sites where many internet users go during their time online.

Portals are locations where internet customers log into the internet. America Online is perhaps the largest of these. Therefore, advertisements tend to be concentrated at these points because these tend to be the opening screen an internet user sees when first going into the internet.

Cyberatlas recently conducted a survey of the distribution of internet users that go through major portals. As you can see in Figure S1–1, Yahoo, Excite, and Alta Vista dominate this area. Only a few gathering places can be identified on the internet.

Outside of portals and communities, the users of the internet tend to scatter. A Florida State University study (*Beyond Demographics: Motivations of World-Wide Web Users and Their Implications for the Future of Advertising,* Robert Riley Jr., 1997) found that internet users enjoy being able to explore the internet and control the level of advertising they experience. The key to making a sale to internet users was to exploit this exploratory behavior, not to use traditional broadcast marketing techniques.

2. *The internet is just like other technologies.*

Just like television, the telephone, bulk mail, and other means of advertising and securing sales, the internet is only a new technology and medium. It is not unique from other media. The internet can transmit

Figure S1–1. Domination of Portals

Portal	Percent of Traffic
Yahoo!	45.92%
Excite	21.68%
Alta Vista	9.70%
Infoseek	5.32%
Web Crawler	3.35%
HotBot	3.42%
Snap	3.09%

sales messages and take orders. Its difference lies in its huge size and dynamic nature.

3. *Customers need a level of trust before they purchase.*

Repeated studies found that a level of trust must exists between an internet customer and the commerce web site before a purchase would result. This includes studies like those conducted by the Year 2000 project at Vanderbilt University.

4. *Customers have distinct likes and dislikes about the internet.*

The University of Ulster Survey on Electronic Information Commerce by Paul Kingsley was a comprehensive look at the likes and dislikes of the internet audience. They found that their respondents ranked as very important (by percentage) the following factors listed in Figure S1–2.

Figure S1–2. Consumer Preferences about the Internet

Factor Which Increases Value of Information on the Internet	Percentage Saying It was very Important
Up to date contents	67.7
Can be downloaded quickly	58.2
Cheaper than print	36.6
Lots of links to other sites	28.3
Contents more relevant than print	32.7
Prints contents as they appear on the screen	26.9
Greater quantity than print	26.6
Presents information not possessed by others	24.0
Sent by e-mail	21.2
Secure and convenient payment methods	25.9
Helps with an educational course	16.8
Saves physical storage space	19.6
Publisher has academic credentials	14.7
It will make money for you	13.4
Publisher has a respected name	6.2
It has high quality graphics	8.4
Desktop publishing quality of web page	6.4

There are many implications in this study. We begin to see the need for trust in a web site for it to have "value." We see that the ability to find new information is very important. We also see that the overall presentation quality of the web page is not as important as you might suspect.

A Forrester Research's Media Field Study found that internet users like web sites with strong content and frequent updates of information. The loading time of the web page had to be fast with the information presented in an easy to read and navigate style. Users found new sites mostly through search engines, e-mail notices, external links, and word of mouth. Ineffective were branding, cutting edge technology, chat rooms, and banner advertisements.

The Redsquare Group in the United Kingdom found that internet users liked the idea that the internet had such a wide variety of things to discover. They enjoyed the idea of important information being at their fingertips. The 24-hour a day availability was also enjoyed. Dislikes were slow web pages, bad navigation, spam e-mail, and failing to find needed information.

5. *The potential for the internet is huge.*

To begin with, the average internet user is older, more educated, and has more disposable income than an average "customer." There is also a balance in the number of men and women that use the internet.

Average age of users: 35.2 years*

Income: 42% above $50,000 a year* 58% above $40,000**

Education: 18% Post Graduate
            23% College Graduate
            32% Some College
            27% High School or less*

Sources: *Cyberatlas   **Georgia Tech GVU studies

The average internet user spends four hours a week on the internet. This time is being taken away from television viewing. At the same time, the number of internet users is expected to grow to one billion by 2003 (Figure S1–3). Estimates vary, but the most conservative is that

Figure S1-3. Predicted Number of Internet Users

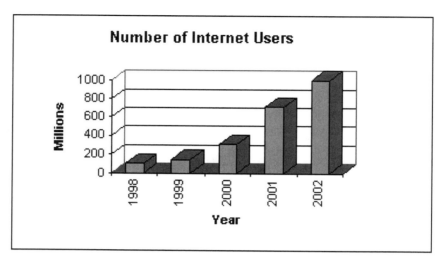

half a trillion dollars will be exchanged on the internet within five years (Figure S1–4).

An IntelliQuest study indicated that the online stores listed in Figure S1–5 were making the greatest impact on the internet. Interesting, there were leaders but very few competitors that seemed to be able to compete against these leaders.

It was the team's job to find out why these sites were so effective. Using the previous study results it was quick to see that these sites provided a valuable service, had current information, and were easy to use and navigate.

Another interesting discovery was the effect of the MP3 music compression algorithm on a sales industry. MP3 allows music to be compressed in CD quality and sent quickly over the internet. Musical groups quickly discovered that they could record their songs and sell them directly to customers on the internet. The traditional functions in the music industry of record labels, distributions channels, promotion, and retail outlets were all circumvented. This was an early and important clue to the success of selling on the internet.

Figure S1-4. Revenue Expected from the Internet

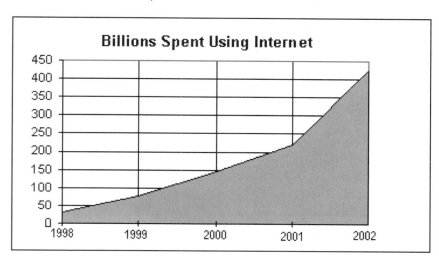

The other observation came from Solution Specialists interviewing people that used eBay. It was quickly discovered that several local businesses had shut their doors and moved all sales activities to the internet. The most telling of these was a specialty card shop that used unique paper stock to print cards. The retail store lost $50,000 the year before the storefront was closed. The first year on the internet resulted in a

Figure S1-5. Dominant Web Sites and Their Products

Web Site	Product
amazon.com	books, etc.
Cdnow.com	music
microsoft.com	software
dell.com	hardware
gap.com	clothing
aol.com, yahoo.com, travelocity.com (tie)	travel services

profit of just over $250,000. Several retail computer hardware stores reported similar results.

Observations like these are very nice for studies, but they eventually have to be translated into tactics to have practical value. This was the next task for the study group.

Additional information on internet trends can be found at the following sites.

www.findsvp.com
www2000.ogsm.vanderbilt.edu
www.cc.gatech.edu/gvu/user_surveys
www.cyberatlas.com
www.cyberdialog.com
www.nua.ie/surveys

The Sales Potential of the Internet

The studies conducted previously demonstrated that the internet has great potential. This, then, begs the question of why so many e-commerce sites fail to deliver on this potential? The problem lays with companies failing to take an organized and disciplined approach to the problem.

In many cases we have seen companies get carried away with software and hardware issues when establishing e-commerce. "The site has to be world-class, we want tons of ordering features, we've got to design our own custom database," and so on. Instead, all of our studies indicated that off-the-shelf software, plain web sites without add-ons, and common-sense were the most efficient choices. Effectiveness was gained by handling e-commerce the same as any other marketing effort. Goals and objectives should be set, tactics adopted based on the study of your target audience, and sales efforts coordinated so that the process of creating a sale goes smoothly for the customer.

At the same time, every sales professional must realize that the internet and its audience is unique. The environment is open and wild. Few rules can be applied. The audience has specific likes and dislikes. By delivering what the audience enjoys while avoiding the dislikes, you position your sales effort for success. To be successful you have to use a sales model that works. All our tests were based on the traditional model of sales.

How to sell on the internet

What cannot be sold on the internet? The answer is "almost nothing." And, therefore, the great fear among sales and marketing professionals is that the internet is going to put them out of a job. The following sections will show you why the internet is a new career opportunity and not the threat you might believe. A quick illustration can be made to show why this is so. The music compression utility MP3 enables a musician to sell CD quality copies of his or her music directly to the public over the internet. This eliminates the need for record stores, record companies, and distribution houses. It also eliminates the need for all associated sales and marketing people. Or does it?

Bruce Springsteen might have the ability to sell a new song directly to you, but does he have the personal time for a full sales and marketing program? Not likely. He needs sales and marketing people familiar with the internet and how it works as a sales tool to support such distribution. The retail record stores need advice on how to compete against realities like MP3. The record companies need a new marketing strategy that embraces the internet's possibilities.

The internet merely changes the environment of selling and marketing. It does not change the rules and skills that make a sales professional effective. It does provide a whole new channel for marketing efforts. Simply stated, it provides many more opportunities than it does threats. IS managers need to teach this reality to their sales and marketing departments.

How to sell in the real world

Marketing is the combination of several activities such as making your product known to the public, creating sales leads, identifying potential customers, defining your market, and studying competitors. Later we will show you how, as an IS manager, you can match the marketing potential of the largest corporations.

For right now, we want to start with how to sell a product or service. The traditional model throughout history has been:

1. Contact potential customers.
2. Build a relationship with interested customers.
3. Make your presentation.
4. Close the sale.
5. Establish customer relationship management.

Contacting potential customers means that either you meet customers at a retail location, you are given sales leads to follow-up on, or you have to generate these leads before you can make contact. Today, the internet gives you the ability to tap huge markets of potential customers.

Once you contact a potential customer, you have very little time to catch their attention and start to build a positive relationship. It is very helpful to know the "serious" buyers from the "might be interested" crowd. That way you can focus your relationship building on the best potential customers. A key part of that relationship building is to establish some degree of trust. This level is determined by the situation and the type of product involved.

The presentation is your chance to show off your product and service. You want to highlight the key features that would be of greatest interest to your customer. Effective relationship building will determine the customer's needs and problems before and during the presentation. The best approach is to present your product as the solution to a problem the customer has identified. All presentations should end with the request to close the deal.

Once the deal is negotiated you close the sale. This includes determining model, color, service length, and a host of other details. It is also an opportunity to show the strength your company has in meeting specific customer needs while effectively fulfilling the order. Being able to ship overnight, get the requested vehicle quickly, provide no-questions asked return policies, good warranty coverage, and other features helps to conclude the sale while building customer loyalty.

Recently, it has been pointed out that repeat business is critical in many sales situations. As such, the sales professional is crucial in providing the liaison between the company and the customers. Handling customers complaints quickly and effectively can ensure repeat business and repeat commissions.

The type of business you are in, the products or services you represent will determine the exact way you use this model. For the individual sales or marketing professional, the following material can help them jump-start your effective entry into internet based selling. For the sales and marketing department of companies this same material will help them to formulate an effective strategy of increasing sales through the internet. For businesses wishing to sell more over the internet, this material will also provide you with the information you need to be a strong competitor. As IS manager, this is your training material. You need to be the e-commerce strategy team leader.

Using conventional sales tactics on the internet

The conventional sales model can be used on the internet. The difference lies in the expectations of the audience on the internet. The internet is a world-wide network of computers and human knowledge. Within a few years over one billion people will be using the internet. This represents a staggeringly large potential market for you and your products. Unfortunately, it also represents a large population of competitors, scam artists, and negative impressions you will have to fight through to succeed.

Some internet statistics

The average user of the internet tends to be older, better educated, and wealthier than the general population. For a long time it used to be mostly males using the internet but that trend has been reversed and an even balance of males and females is now reality.

More and more people are using interactive services as an important tool for making their lives easier and more convenient. In fact, a majority of those who have shopped on-line say its the easiest way to make purchases. Nearly three-quarters of the on-line consumer population say they go on-line to get information about products to buy.

The America Online/Roper Starch Cyberstudy of 1998 found that nearly two-thirds of Internet customers who have been online three or more years now view the internet as a necessity to their lives. That's quite remarkable, given that a few years ago not many people were using the internet and most of them thought it was a novelty. The future will most likely be a more serious use of the internet for selling.

Nearly 90% of all online consumers say they would miss the internet if it were no longer available to them, and more than three-quarters believe internet services have made their lives better. If stranded on a desert island, two-thirds of surveyed consumers indicated that they would prefer to have a computer with an internet connection. Only 23% wanted a telephone and 9% wanted a television. In short, the internet is the new media of marketing and the new direction for sales.

Using the internet for sales and marketing

What you need to do is to learn and use new and effective ways to use the internet as part of your sales and marketing efforts. As you shall see later, sales and marketing will blend into each other on the internet. You can be taking orders while, at the same time, building brand recognition or announcing a new product. In fact, we are going to show you how to use the internet to create wholly new products and services to expand your markets. To use the internet effectively you need to first understand the needs and expectations of your internet customers.

Expectations of internet customers

The typical customer will see the internet as a worldwide connection to knowledge and resources. The idea of being able to buy, sell, and auction on the internet is a growing realization. Delays, failures, and other problems with the internet are expected but not enjoyed. Internet customers worry about the security of the information they give out, especially credit card information.

What they like:

- being connected to a whole world of new people, places, ideas, and possibilities
- easy navigation around web sites
- polite, well-written e-mail
- quick order fulfillment, including good return policies
- brand recognition
- free advice, literature, software, etc.
- assurance of security with the information they give out

- up-to-date information and technology
- clean, easy-to-read presentations

What they dislike:

- "spam" e-mail (the equivalent of junk mail)
- hard to navigate web sites
- shady deals, questionable ethics and internet practices
- slow response times
- getting nothing back for visiting a web site

If we go back to our model of selling with these expectations in mind, we can begin to build a sales and marketing presence on the internet and assure great effectiveness. We will show you exactly how to meet the positive expectations of internet customer, build a relationship of trust, make your presentation, close the sale, fulfill the order, and establish customer relationship management.

The traditional approach to the internet

Most of the literature you read about doing business on the internet talks about setting up a web site, creating order forms, and listing your site on internet search engines. This is sound advice that is not effective without further actions. This is where you will start. However, we are also going to show you that your web site and e-mail can be used differently to create leads, build relationships, make presentations, and close sales.

The bottom line: an overview of the rules to use

1. Professional sales and marketing efforts are respected as much on the internet as they are in the real world.
2. There is no time or space on the internet. A single sales professional can have the effectiveness of an entire sales organization.
3. You need the right plan, the right people, and the right tools to succeed. We will show you how to get all three.

4. The key strategy is to either form an internet community, or be closely associated with an established community.

Review of the rules

- The internet represents one of the fastest-growing opportunities for sales and marketing. If used correctly, the internet is very effective for sales and marketing.
- The traditional model of selling still applies to the internet. You need to build a relationship with your customers, discover their needs, and present your product or service as the answer to their problems.
- Understanding the subtle differences of the internet from other sales and marketing media is critical to your success.
- Knowing the expectations of the internet community will form the basis for the methods we are about to teach you.

Lesson One: The Customer Comes First

It has been noted that repeat business is critical in many sales situations. As such, the sales professional is critical in providing the liaison between the company and the customers. Handling customers' complaints quickly and effectively can ensure repeat business and repeat commissions. The type of business you are in and the products or services you represent will determine the exact way you use this model. Let's look at a couple of examples.

Example 1: buying a car

Automobiles are one of the largest purchases people make. The dealership might use advertising, letters, cold calls, and word of mouth to make contact with potential customers. Eventually the customer comes into the showroom and meets the sales representative face to face. The first few minutes are critical to building a relationship with that customer. Building trust in the car business is very difficult. The sales representative then presents several models to the customer and discusses the customer's specific needs. Another critical point is asking for the sale. When done correctly after building a good relationship, the customer can be convinced to make the purchase. The sale is closed, money exchanged, and the sales representative assures delivery and reviews how to drive and take care of the new vehicle. If done correctly, all of this will generate good word of mouth and future sales.

Car and Driver magazine recently reported the case of a man wishing to purchase either a Corvette, a BMW, or a Lexus. He went to the Corvette dealer first. Here he learned that he couldn't test drive the car, there was a waiting list, and he would have to take whatever color came in. At BMW they were glad to have him drive the car, the color he wanted could be obtained in a few weeks, and the manual transmission would cost thousands more. At Lexus, he got the color he wanted with a manual transmission the same day, the sales department was willing to negotiate the price, and he could test drive it all he wanted.

It is no surprise that he bought the Lexus. However, what happened next illustrates the proper approach to internet sales techniques. As they handed him the keys they told him to forget washing or fueling the car for the first year, they would take care of that for him at no charge. He was also put through a half-day class on how to take care of the car and drive it effectively. The next day he got flowers at the office as a thank you for purchase. Several managers at the dealership sent personal letters thanking him for the purchase and offering their help if he ever needed it. Which car will this customer think about recommending in the future? It looks like he already did and in a national magazine.

This is what we mean by the "force multiplying" effect of the internet. This story on the internet would have reached tens of thousands of interested car buyers that could have e-mailed the man involved to confirm his story. Think about the marketing potential of that scenario.

Example 2: buying insurance

When it comes time to select auto insurance for that new car, the customer can either go to the physical office of an insurance agent, call around for quotes, or use the internet to search for the best policy at a fair price. This time the marketing efforts of the insurance companies play a big part in making their brand of insurance recognizable to the customer. It also helps to build trust in particular companies. Once the customer contacts the insurance company for a quote, the relationship building process begins. Agents that are helpful and can communicate clearly do very well. More trust is built and the sale is made. It is not unusual for the customer and the agent to never see each other face-to-face.

The success of insurance companies with virtually no sales agents in the field demonstrates that both telephone and internet-based sales and marketing practices can be very efficient. These two examples illustrate how the sales model works, but they also show that if you build the right relationship with customers and can establish the right level of trust, you can make the sale.

Sales and marketing

The point of this chapter is to look at the new and effective ways to use the internet as part of your sales and marketing efforts. As we shall see in Chapter 2, sales and marketing will blend into each other on the internet. You can be taking orders while at the same time building brand recognition or announcing a new product. In fact, we are going to show you how to use the internet to create wholly new products and services and expand your markets.

Lesson Two: The Traditional Internet Sales Model Is Ineffective

Most of the literature you read about doing business on the internet talks about setting up a web site, creating order forms, and listing your site on internet search engines. We witnessed one client that was able to have a considerable impact on the internet without a web site. With over three million e-commerce sites now on the internet, we would expect a larger number of success stories and an even larger flow of money. Neither is in evidence. Profitable e-commerce sites for large corporations are few.

The Bottom Line: An Overview of the Basic Internet Selling Principles

1. The internet represents one of the fastest growing opportunities for sales and marketing. If used incorrectly, the internet is not effective for sales. When used correctly it can force-multiply your sales efforts.

2. The traditional model of selling still applies to the internet. You need to build a relationship with your customers.

3. Understanding the subtle differences of the internet from other sales and marketing media is critical to your success.

4. Knowing the expectations of the internet community and meeting those needs creates the opportunity for success.

5. Discipline is critical to the effort. Skip a step or fail to dedicate enough resources and the effect is diminished.

Formulating an Internet Sales Plan

Any sales effort requires a plan. You need to know your own resources and capabilities. You need to know the position and capabilities of your competitors. Then you need your plan of attack. Traditional wisdom on internet sales takes one of two forms. The first is the idea of getting a web site built, putting an order form on the site, listing your site on a lot of search engines, running banner ads, and then sitting back and waiting for sales to pour in. This is also called the "dressed for failure" model.

It fails on three important points. There are over three million other commerce sites on the internet and almost all follow this model. Therefore, there is nothing to distinguish the site. Without proper content, few people will find or stay at this site. The submission to a search engine will list you deep into hundreds of other sites. Most importantly, there is no customer management going on in this model. Relationships aren't being built and after-sales activities are non-existent.

The second common approach to internet-based sales is to establish a unique site with important information for potential customers that is updated frequently. Click-through advertisements at large search engine sites direct traffic to your page. Links are established with many other sites so that more people can discover the site. An easy to use catalog of items available is presented, orders can be taken and confirmed on the internet or by phone, and a small staff maintains contact with existing customers.

This is called the "somewhat successful" model. Some of these sites do fairly well and others don't break even. The problem here is that the site is still static. The sales strategy revolves around a web site that doesn't move.

The attention to good content and constant contact with potential and existing customers is very wise. However, you need to go out and draw people into your site, not wait for links and ads to bring them in. For example, the effectiveness of click-through ads diminishes every year. People just don't notice them as much anymore. And, there is no rule that says you can have just one web site.

So, what do you do to create a truly effective sales plan? The answer is that you use your new knowledge of the expectations of the internet to your advantage.

In the internet world there is no time or space. You can launch entire marketing and sales campaigns in a matter of seconds. In fact, rapid activity is highly recommended on the internet. Therefore, your plan must be based on two ideas, getting good information out to the audience fast, and build a community where people come by habitually, instead of being driven to your site. The trust built in a community will promote more sales than either of the methods discussed above.

There are some basic rules you want to keep in mind when planning your internet campaign.

1. Build a community.
2. Give something away for free.
3. Establish trust with your customers by being prompt and professional.
4. Follow the sales model, relationship first, then presentation, then the sale.
5. Always follow-up with customers.
6. All presentations should be clean, neat, and to-the-point.

Build a community

The best way to maximize your performance on the internet is to establish a community. A community is a place where people of similar interest gather on the internet. Take a look at the Pentax site (www.pentax.com). Here camera users gather to discuss how to use Pentax equipment. There are plenty of photographic interest sites on the internet, but only this one dedicated to a particular brand of camera.

Note how the engineers from Pentax are freely participating in the discussions. They are being helpful and honest. There is no sales pitch going on here. Therefore, the users of this site can feel comfortable being there. As they enter and exit, however, they pass by the Pentax information pages. When they are ready to purchase they know where to find the presentation and price. When they need advice, they have people they can talk to.

Therefore, you need to study the market you are in. Do you sell chemicals to industry, luxury cars to the public, condos in the Bahamas, software to lawyers? Whatever you sell you have an audience. You need to know the interests of that audience. You need to find out what information they need that no one else provides. This is one way to build your community, by providing that information.

Give something away for free

Practically every internet user loves the idea of getting something for free from an internet site. Hewlett-Packard gives away their printer driver software, Turner Entertainment gives away the monthly viewing guide to the Turner Movie Classic Channel, CNNfn provides up to the minute stock quotes. Other sites give away newsletter subscriptions, e-mail discussions, tips and techniques, font of the day, joke of the day, and a host of other interesting pieces of information.

An effective internet sales campaign will focus on finding the pieces of information, software, or opportunity for chatting that motivates repeat visits to your site. Once you find this, your community begins to build itself. Your promotional efforts focus on the services and free items you provide. For example, the sales team for a pharmaceutical company posts a free e-mail update service on the legislation to allow pharmacists greater freedom to dispense medical advice. This is a "hot-button" issue to the audience of potential customers.

Establish trust with your customers by being prompt and professional

We cannot say enough about the importance of always appearing and acting professional on the internet. You will probably never be seen live by your customers, but the quality of your e-mail language, the effective design of your web site, the ease of navigation you provide, and the promptness in responding to customer inquiries will make the difference between success and failure on the internet.

Later we will advise you to keep your e-mail running all of the time with auto-responders to make sure that any customer inquiry is promptly handled. We will also stress the importance of the proper way to compose e-mail for customers.

Follow the sales model: relationship first, then presentation, then the sale

The internet is full of the most skittish customers in the world. They shy quickly from "salesmen." You are the provider of information and the offering point for products. Pushing products on the internet rarely works. Instead, you strictly follow the traditional sales model. Once a customer reaches you by e-mail or visits your site the first information presented should be for the purposes of building a relationship.

On your web site you explain who you are and who you represent. Testimonies and obvious links to the free items come first. What follows are invitations on every page for the viewer to browse your product descriptions. This will be the gentle transformation from meeting the customer, learning their needs, and making the presentation.

Always follow-up with customers

Whether a potential or existing customer, you always answer inquiries. If a potential customer asks you to fax him a catalog, do so. You do not tell them to "look at the one at our web site." If a customer that purchases your product has a complaint, offer to mediate the conclusion they would like to see on their behalf, do not transfer the e-mail to the manufacturer.

Once a purchase has been made, send a thank you note via e-mail. People love to get these. A few times a year send a follow up message to all customers letting them know of the new products you have to offer or discounts your are offering this week. Let them know they are getting the announcement ahead of the published sales announcement. Notify a customer of any updates or upgrades that become available for the product they bought. In short, do everything possible to keep the customer happy so that they return for more purchases and recommend you to other potential customers.

All presentations should be clean, neat, and to-the-point

Any e-mail, web site, discussion list, faxed item, written letter, or other form of communications with the customer should be neat and clean. Don't use fancy graphics, movies, or sounds on your web site unless they represent the product directly. Do use white space generously and make navigation between pages easy. Do format e-mail to match a professional sales letter.

Even more important to internet customers, get right to the point when communicating with the audience. The internet audience is very impatient. They are used to jumping to many sites and quickly scanning the information. The shorter your message, the better.

More thoughts for your plan

We have already seen that the audience on the internet has a set of expectations you will not find anywhere else. Therefore, when using the skills we are about to teach you, you need to keep these expectation constantly in mind. The same holds true in establishing your strategic sales plan.

1. What is the current sales plan outside the internet?
2. What will be our sales presence?
3. What audience is our target?
4. What outcomes do we expect to achieve?

By gathering the traditional information from market research you build the framework for your strategic plans. Knowing what the customer needs and expects, as well as whether your competitors provide these needs and expectations, is critical to planning your attack.

Lesson Three: Use the Right People

When we talk about having the right people to be a successful internet sales site, we are talking about finding the right people to help you in your efforts.

Internally, you will have your sales staff and sales support personnel. They need to be retrained on the potential of the internet and the new approaches being used to take advantage of this new sales territory.

The internal sales staff will have to know how to connect to the internet, process e-mail, and monitor web sites. These are the minimal skills for sales people supporting your efforts. Depending on their role in the strategic plan, they may also have to learn how to update web pages, use sales contact software, operate personal digital assistants, and any other support skill required to respond to incoming customer inquiries.

Internet service providers

Externally, you will need to find and form working relationships with several groups of people. The first will be your internet service provider (ISP). The ISP sets up the connection between either you or your company and the internet. With this connection comes services such as e-mail, web pages, e-commerce sites, and the like.

In large companies, the ISP provides dedicated data lines between the company and the internet. These are hooked to computers at your company that create the e-mail, web page, database, and other internet services. Either way, the ISP is a critical link in the process. They are responsible for keeping the connection to the internet up and running. They also should provide training and technical support to keep your team well-informed and running smoothly.

Web page designers

We have previously seen that the ease of use of a web page, especially navigation between pages, is critical to internet sales success. Learning to be an excellent web page builder and designer takes considerable time and effort. As IS manager, your job is to coordinate. Therefore, you will want to find and work with a web page designer with a proven track record of attractive and easy to use sites.

When working with this person, you lay out the way you want your product to be presented on a web page. The web page designer will ask a series of questions on functionality, where you want e-mail leads sent, how you will update the page, and so on. For a flat fee they will create the web page that can be anything from a simple presentation of product to a major community site or storefront on the internet. The cost of such services start at a few hundred dollars and goes up according to the size and complexity of the project.

Always be sure to look at previous work done by a prospective web page designer. Talk to the companies that have used this person before. Make sure projects are done swiftly and accurately. In addition, the designer will need to talk to your ISP to get details on how pages are loaded into the system and how to restrict access for updating.

Technical support

The internet and all internet sales activities seem to rely on the use of computers and software. These are products known for their ability to create unique and frustrating problems. Data can move or vanish, modems don't talk to the internet, access is suddenly restricted, hard drives crash, and a host of other possibilities. Remember, your job is to coordinate. If a problem takes more than a few moments to solve, then call the technical support people.

There should be a technical support line for your computers, maybe another for the software packages, and more technical support phone numbers for the ISP. Therefore, you want to take the time to learn about the technical support capabilities of each source of help. When you purchase a computer, the technical support that is offered as part of the package should be investigated and tested. The same is true of ISPs and software.

Ask if support is available around the clock. What is the cost of asking questions? How fast will a response come? What level of success can be expected? What alternatives are there when a problem can't be solved? How large of an experience database does the technical staff possess? These are all questions to ask before you commit to a technical support service.

Researchers, marketers, and others

Depending upon the extent of your sales efforts on the internet, you may have to enlist other professional services to help you. For example, suppose you need research done on the preferences of people 30 to 45 years of age earning over $50,000 a year in the United States. Market research companies probably have such information available. To save time you spend money to have a professional researcher find the best data at the lowest price.

If you need to test your product for features that appeal to various customers, then the marketing professionals can help. The same is true of advertising professionals that would know the best way to get increased recognition of the brand of your product and the name of your web site. In short, save your time for coordination and implementation. Use professionals under contract or borrowed from other departments to assist you with the critical points in your sales site strategy.

Lesson Four: Use the Right Tools

Electronic mail

Electronic mail (e-mail) is the lynch pin that holds together your approach to selling on the internet. Virtually every customer contact involving the internet will be done through e-mail. You will need a strong internal policy on the use of e-mail when contacting customers. Let's look a little deeper at the right way to use e-mail. The rules, as we have presented them, are simple:

1. Use the same level of formality you would in any business letter to create a professional image.
2. Internet people are in a hurry to get information so respond quickly with short, to-the-point messages and replies.
3. Never make a direct sales pitch in the first e-mail sent to a potential customer. The internet is very anonymous and people like to build up some feeling of trust before being approached to buy something. Therefore, you use the first two or three e-mails to build a relationship with the customer. You can mention that a product is available, but don't "push" for the sale up front.
4. The fourth rule is to respond quickly. People expect instant results from the internet and they frequently get it. Therefore, as fast as possible, answer any e-mail inquiries.
5. Link your e-mail with your customer database.

Personalization is a very effective sales technique on the internet. Therefore, the fifth rule says that you should link your e-mail with your customer database software. That way you can quickly look up what communications have already been sent by your company to a prospective customer. By mentioning details like, ". . . as we discussed last week, discounts are available . . ." you make the prospective customer feel as if they have your undivided attention. That builds trusts and makes for more sales.

Speak directly to customers

This leads to the sixth and final rule—always speak to a customer as if they are the only person you are talking to. This is an expansion on the idea of personalizing your communications via e-mail. In fact, this is a big part of building a "community" on the internet. If you start an e-mail with . . .

> "Mr. Jones, it is so good to hear from you again after our last correspondence on May 15th. I hope your wife is feeling better."

This shows that you remembered when you last received e-mail from Mr. Jones and that he mentioned his response was late on May 15th because his wife had to have minor surgery. This kind of personal touch to a potentially impersonal technology like e-mail builds a relationship and a community.

Examples to study

Like its counterpart, the business letter, there are rules to follow when using e-mail. Your company staff must act like the professional sales people when composing or answering e-mail.

Example of good and bad e-mail   E-mail will be used in several situations under your general sales strategy. For example, you may have a web page that encourages the browsing audience to "send an e-mail to have your questions answered." A customer may send an e-mail saying,

> "I see that you offer three-year extended warranties on your product. What does that cost?
>
> Fred Caller"

Notice how this potential customer is asking a direct question. No mention is made of what product he might be interested in or whether a purchasing decision has been made. The signature is simple with no title or company name. Your job is to compose a quick response that will draw out some of this information.

One possible way to do this would be the following reply. First you would check your customer database file and see if Mr. Caller has contacted you or the company before. If so, you would make reference to the previous contacts to let Mr. Caller know that you are aware of former conversations. If not, you should begin with an introduction, like this,

> "Mr. Caller,
>
> Thank you for your e-mailed question. My name is Frank Terms, sales representative for AXZ corporation. The extended warranties vary in price according to the item(s) you purchase. For example, a three-year warranty for the Phoneplex Unit is $329 U.S. Most contracts are in the $295 to $459 range with discounts available. If you have a particular model in mind or you want a set of units I can give you a free, no-obligation quote. Feel free to call me at 616-555-9114 or e-mail to Frank@sales.wids.net.
>
> Frank Terms, Sales Rep.
> AXZ Corporation
> www.wids.net
> 'Building trust, one customer at a time' "

Note how Mr. Terms did not press for a sale. Instead he starts with the formality of an introduction to make Mr. Caller feel that a relationship is being built. Mr. Terms will call Fred "Mr. Caller" until invited to do otherwise. The direct question has been answered in a way to encourage further conversation. A free, no-obligation quote is offered. This is part of the "give the customer something free" rule we introduced earlier. Finally, Mr. Terms offers both phone number and e-mail for response. This gives Mr. Caller more comfort knowing that he can always pick up the phone and talk to someone right away.

You should also note the ending signature that gives the name of the company and its web page address. This is usually linked automatically by

Mr. Caller's e-mail program so that a simple click of the mouse will take Mr. Caller to the AXZ web page. That allows Mr. Caller to quickly check which products he may be interested in purchasing.

Mr. Terms will link this e-mail and response to his customer database. If Mr. Caller does not respond, this could indicate a non-potential customer. A polite follow-up e-mail may be called for to make sure. A rapid response would likely mean you have an interested customer. A slow response indicates a customer in need of a little coaxing.

Second example Ms. Sally Fortune is the internet sales representative for Break-Away Vacation Travel. She is in charge of finding new customers for this travel service company. She is new to e-mail and attempts to use the language of bulk-faxed promotions in an e-mail. See if you can spot many of the mistakes in this approach.

"Corporate Sellout

BAHAMAS CRUISE AND ISLAND VACTION FOR ONLY $79.99

*First 50 e-mail in responses
*Round trip with all meals included
*3 Days, 2 Nights at a famous resort on the Grand Bahamas Island

First come, first serve, call 800-367-5454

Sally Fortune
Marketing Director
Sally@travel.com"

Luckily, Sally's boss, Norma, reviewed this e-mail. Here are just some of the problems.

1. Internet people hate obvious and pushy sales promotions they didn't ask for.
2. The e-mail looks like "spam" where a single sales message is sent to millions of internet users.
3. Professionalism wasn't established in the message.

4. Using capital letters in e-mail is like shouting.

5. No relationship building is taking place.

6. The reader is being directed to a 800 phone number and not return e-mail plus a phone number.

See if you can think of others. In the meantime, let's look at the second attempt that uses our rules of e-mail for selling.

"Mr. Yates,

Excuse me for the interruption. My name is Sally Fortune. You once indicated on our web page that you wish to receive travel information about the Bahamas as it became available. Break-Away Travel has just received a set of 50 tickets for a 3-day, 2-night Bahamas vacation for $79.99, including meals and travel. I thought that this might be of interest to you. If so, let me know by return e-mail or please feel free to call me at 800-367-5454, extension 25. I would be happy to hold as many slots as you may need. If this message reached you by error, just send me a quick e-mail to that effect and I will make sure that you are removed from our notification list.

Thanks again, Sally"

Notice how this e-mail still tells about the travel opportunity and takes care to be very polite with Mr. Yates. Only specific people that have asked for notification are contacted. If a bulk e-mail list is used, the person's name is inserted in the message to make it personal. It also makes it clear that the name can be easily removed from future messages. This makes the internet customer comfortable knowing that he is in control.

Where and how to use e-mail

Looking back at your strategic plan for the internet you can see that e-mail will play an important part in the following:

1. Generating sales leads

2. Keeping in touch with existing and potential customers.

3. Facilitating rapid response to questions.

4. Building a relationship with each customer.
5. Making sales presentations.
6. Asking for the sale.
7. Customer Relationship Management.

Practice your use of e-mail with a small group of customers to get the "feel" of how this is done. In the following chapter we are going to introduce several tools for greater sales effectiveness. Notice how many of these rely on e-mail.

Third example—facilitating rapid response to questions The main advantage of the internet is that you can send lots of information in a hurry to a customer. For example, sales brochures, order forms, photos of the product, and other sales literature can be sent in a few minutes to anyone in the world, at any time.

For now, be aware that your customer contact database software has to be up and running along with your e-mail program at all times. This will not only allow you to know how to respond to each request as it is received, but will allow you to build a collection of standard responses. This will include various versions of your sales literature tailored to particular types of customers.

Let's see what such a response might look like:

"Ms. Hooper,

I just got your e-mail a few minutes ago. Sorry about the delay in responding but I wanted to make sure we have the best fix to recommend for your situation. The technical people indicate that you can turn off the heat sensor for a couple of days without any danger. However, it is critical that someone gets in the machine and fixes that thermostat. I have dispatched Larry Cuke from our Chicago office. He should be there tomorrow at noon. His e-mail is Larry@fixit.com. You can also call him on his cell phone at 312-555-6789. I will call you tomorrow afternoon to make sure that the problem is fixed."

In many situations, your company is expected to help your customers with related problems. A good software sales representative drops off recent patches and provides tips to staff members at a customer's site with each visit. In that way, you are seen as a valuable asset and not "just the sales rep." E-mail can be used to also accomplish this goal.

See how our response denotes actions being taken to respond to the customer's problem? This reassures the customer. A well-solved problem will build customer relationships. A problem not handled can destroy the relationship and cost you potential customers from the bad reputation you develop.

Special Note: *If you offer technical support through your web site, always link the customer directly to the correct fix. Do not tell them to "consult the technical support area on the web page." Instead, say something such as "You can get your new printer to work with our software by downloading the printer driver at:*

www.technical.axz.com/drv3002.htm."

Or better still, "You will need our new print driver to get your new printer to work with our software. I have attached the necessary file to this message. Let me know if you have the slightest problem."

Fourth example—building a relationship with each customer

Relationship building on the internet takes time, effort, and a consistent approach throughout your internet presence. For e-mail, that means you use business letter formality and proven methods for written sales pitches. You want your customer to recognize that you are running a professional and reliable internet site. This has to be shown in the quality of your writing and that of all members of your company's sales team. Learning how to write short and effective sales letters is a valuable skill on the internet. Later techniques, such as managed mailing lists, can be used to further promote your image and promote a relationship.

We looked at relationship building on first contact earlier. Now let's look at how a follow-up e-mail might be worded:

"Ms. Token,

Thank you for your request for further information on our line of well drilling equipment. Your e-mail indicated that you need to drill about a thousand feet through a mostly sandstone bedrock.

Auger bits #437 and #438 have been used successfully in similar situations with great success. Naturally, I am assuming a drill rate of 150 feet per day. At such a rate you would burn out at most one of the bits. However, there is also the alternative of using a #866 sand and mud bit for the first 100 feet to set up a better casement for more stable drilling at deeper depths. Would that be a concern of yours?

Attached is the quote for either the #437 or #438 bits . . ."

Again, the message is kept short. Notice how standard relationship building methods are still being used here. The customer's concern in the first e-mail is repeated to assure Ms. Token that you understand her problem. You then respond with the information she needs and a possible alternative. The idea is to try and set up a bit of back and forth discussion to build the relationship. Also, you are demonstrating that you understand drilling and can offer excellent advice.

This ability to provide information to educate the customer is key on the internet. With enough of this information to offer, customer-contact people can become the "internet-based experts." People will come to your web site to get answers. Each person drawn in is a potential customer. Your information and your conversations can then be converted into new products for sell, such as a monthly newsletter. It can also be used to create the free product you give to visitors to your web site, such as a question and answer page that is updated frequently.

Fifth example—making sales presentations The presentation is key to making a sale. This is where your company convinces the potential customer that your product is the right product. To do this you have to show that your product solves the customer's identified problem. The conversations you have had via e-mail and other media should have uncovered the central problem the customer is attempting to solve. Your sales presentation not only lists benefits, it shows clearly how the customer's problem is solved.

Here is an example of a sales presentation within an e-mail:

"Hank,

When you photograph the comet for National Geographic, you will have to balance film speed with final production quality.

You are correct that medium format is the way to go. At ISO 1600 you will get the details you want. The Fuji film is the best bet at $9.88 a roll and Kodak's Press film will also work at $8.99 a roll. The Fuji film will bring out the blue tone of the ion tail. The Kodak will capture the dust tail better. I've got both, refrigerated and fresh. I can get them to you overnight for $8.00 more. Call or e-mail me before 4:00 EST and let me know. Try to guide the camera on a telescope mount with at least 10-minute exposure. If the sky is real dark you can go out to 60 minutes with either film."

The presentation can be made in any of several forms. You can attach photos, specifications, blueprints, testimonials, or whatever works best for your situations. In this case, the presentation revolves around the photographer's basic problem. He has one chance to get a good photo of a comet for a famous magazine. The sales representative presents the best choices in film with information on how well they will work and how to best make the exposure. The value of the advice is worth more than the price of the film. Also, note how the e-mail is worded to give the customer two choices, both resulting in a purchase.

Example 6—asking for the sale   Finally, a sales presentation ends with the request to close the sale. This is a critical point in both face-to-face sales and internet sales. You have to guide the customer towards placing an order without giving the impression that you are "pushy." With e-mail you can attach an order form to the end of the message, link to the order form on your web site, or offer to call the customer to confirm the order. The exact approach will depend upon your situation.

Let's see how the close is done in e-mail:

"Bob,

Looks like the Durango is the truck you want. I can beat your best dealership quote by $1,500 dollars and have it delivered to you within a week. I'll need you to send a $500 earnest payment to start the process. You can send a check, fax over your charge card info using the form below, or use our secure web site."

The best approach is to just ask for the sale. In this case, the $500 holds the vehicle and starts the purchasing process. By getting a small amount up front it makes it easier to get the full amount on delivery, the buyer is now committed.

Example 7—customer relationship management After the product is sold, e-mail can be used to maintain your customer relationship management program. You can send a short e-mail asking how the product is working out. You can respond to warranty or technical support issues. You can also keep the customer informed about new uses, upgrades, modifications, patches, and new products. The relationship you built during the sales portion of communication continues.

Let's look at the example of a warranty claim.

"Mr. Higgins,

Recently I purchased an MP3 player from your web site. After two weeks I get an error code and unreliable playing. What do I do now?

Ken Ticked"

Your reply:

"Mr. Ticked,

I am sending you two things. The first is a new MP3 player so that you don't have to go another day without music. The second is a return postage mailer so that you can send us the faulty player for examination. We are keenly interested in the cause of your problem because failure with these units is so rare. I am also enclosing with your new unit a $10 off coupon for future purchases from our web site to help compensate you for the interruption in your music enjoyment."

Remember, satisfying an annoyed customer can be very good future business for your company. A customer that tells his friends how well he was treated when a problem occurred is better than most advertising campaigns.

Because we are talking about the internet, those positive comments can be spread very far and wide, very fast.

Remember to use names wisely

A critical part in the application process are the name your company staff will use on the internet. Each account name will be attached to e-mail. For example, Bob White signing up with 9000.net will have the e-mail address of:

Bob_White@9000.net

This is fine unless you want to maximize your e-mail address potential. The first part of the address can be anything you want, such as:

Sales@9000.net
Value@9000.net
Bob@9000.net

and so on. Therefore, you also need to consider whether you want a specific domain name on the internet. This is the second half of the e-mail address (9000.net). By choosing carefully you can incorporate your sales presentation into both your e-mail address and web page.

Take the example of automobile dealer selling sports cars on the internet. The maker of the cars has already captured the domain names associated with the vehicles (i.e. BMW.com, MercedesBenz.com, Lexus.com). Therefore, the marketing manager chooses "Funcars" as the account name and domain name. This emphasizes why most people buy a sports car, for fun. Thus, you get e-mail addresses like,

Bob@funcars.com

for the personal touch or,

Sales@funcars.com

for the more professional approach.

Summary

As you can see from the discussion above, a lot of thinking has to go into the sales and marketing aspect of your business before you design the e-commerce site. Implied here is that you need to conduct training for both your staff and the sales staff of your company. As we will see in the next chapter, the construction of an e-commerce site takes quite a bit of work and planning.

Suggested Reading

"The Wired Sales Professional," by the Wired Sales Group, 1999 (available through amazon.com)

Suggested Sites

9000.net—our web site for this book
wiredsales.net—the wired sales group's web site

Suggested Search Terms

c-commerce
internet sales

Chapter S2
Building the
e-Commerce Site

Perhaps the biggest project you are getting handed in your company is e-commerce. Unfortunately, this hot new trend in business is following the same path of most trends. First, a key manager hears the term "e-commerce." Companies like IBM are hawking the benefits of having a commerce site on the internet. Other companies like Amazon.com, cdnow.com, and ebay.com are making what looks like tons of money with very little effort. Therefore, the word goes out from top management, "we must have e-commerce."

The problem is that if you asked them what "e-commerce" means the top managers would be at a loss to explain their goals and objectives. It is more than a web-site on the internet. It can be a variety of tactics and technologies applied to your internet presence. It can involve suppliers and sub-contractors. It can involve internet-only alliances with competitors. It can be a wide variety of things. Without clear targets, goals, and objectives it can be a failure.

As we saw in the previous chapter, without a strong sales and marketing plan that either creates a community or associates with a community the likelihood of success is low. Therefore, you need to work with management, sales, and marketing to first develop your overall sales strategy for the internet. Once you have that, the mechanics of your internet sites falls into place.

Let's take a specific example. Your company sells software to control manufacturing processes. Your customers are manufacturers around the world. Currently you control five percent of the market. Your management would like to control 10% and use the leverage of the internet to get there.

Your strategic meeting with management should define the goals, objectives, targets, and vision of upper management when it comes to e-commerce.

1. Goals are the performance measures used for the project. For example, customers should be able to place an order easily from your web site, new customers should be recruited through the web site, and so on.

2. Objectives are the quantifiable measurements of your goals. For example, the web site should generate at least 10 new customers per month, web hits should be in the thousands, and so on.

3. Targets are the internet positions you wish to capture as part of your conquest of the internet. This includes positions on search engines, links from other sites, and the like.

4. Vision is the look and feel of your internet presence. This is not the look and feel of the web site. It is the customer-focused characteristics of your internet presence, such as e-mail responses within one hour of reception, easy navigation of sites, the free information or service provided by your web site, and so on.

Taken together they give you the strategic picture that you translate into the web sites, mail lists, auction sites, streaming audio/video, or any other internet technology that should be applied. As usual, you use the minimal amount of internet technology to accomplish the goals, objectives, targets, and the vision of the project.

Effective Web Pages

To have an effective web site you need to follow a few simple techniques.

- *The simpler the site, the better.* People like sites that are easy to read.
- *Keep to a direct message.* People want information fast. Clutter in the form of flashing graphics, lots of pictures, and the like are not welcomed.
- *Ease of use.* Your site should be easy to understand and easy to navigate.
- *Easy orders.* A click or two away should be your catalog and order form. Make these easy to use and people will use them.
- *Give something away.* Internet people love to get something for free.
- *Promote return visits.* Constantly updated information, chats about critical data, and new free products keep people coming back to your site.

Selecting the Right Internet Names

Just as important is an appropriate name for your web address. It should be easy to remember, short, and easily associated with your products. For example, www.ibm.com is very much associated with International Business Machines. People should be able to remember your web site name without having to write it down, as in the case of the search engine www.yahoo.com and www.ask.com.

Having a web page is a requirement for internet sales. This is the full-time advertisement, technical support, sales presentation, and order taking site for your product or service. Web pages can also be used to coordinate and train a sales force in the field, provide needed information to sales representatives, and track the success of your internet efforts. In addition, the address of your web page will be on every piece of sales literature you generate.

If we go back to our list of customer expectations in Chapter One, you see that easy navigation, something for free, and good content are key points for any web site. These are sometimes difficult to focus on with the distraction of fancy banners, Java scripts, flashy illustrations, attached sounds, and other "bells and whistles" that can quickly make a page distracting.

Let's look at a few examples to see what effective selling on the internet looks like:

1. eBay (www.ebay.com)—the online auction site allowing direct selling between owner of an item and buyer.
2. Pentax (www.pentax.com)—full information on a line of cameras with an unmoderated discussion of the product by its users.
3. ASR (www.asr.9000.net)- request for quote site competing against really big corporations.
4. Industrial hardware site selling to the OEMs (www.sourcingextranet. net).

If you have never built a web page before, you should either take the time to learn or hire someone to build your page. If you represent a corporation with a single web page but many sales representatives, consult them on whether you can add a page for each sales staff person or the rules you have to use regarding the web pages.

The Web Site

A web site is a collection of related web pages under a single address. The address for web sites are called URLs or Universal Resource Locators. This is a naming convention that routes internet users to your particular web site. For example,

> http://www.voyager.net

takes you to the Voyager ISP web site. Here you can read about the services offered, get technical support, or sign up for an internet account.

The Rules for Web Sites

Once you decide to build a web site you need to follow a few simple rules. Start by going through several web sites of competitors and look for mistakes or repetitive patterns they have made. Avoid these and exploit any weaknesses or omission you find.

1. *Keep it simple.* Use mostly text laid out in an appealing fashion with plenty of white space. If customers come from different countries, offer alternative language versions of the same page.

2. *Keep it direct.* You want to present the minimal amount of information that gets your message across. The best approach is to break the message down into parts that each fit on a short page. For example, the home page (the first one seen by customers) should explain who you are and what's available at this site. Information on specific products would each get a page linked to your order form.

3. *Make it easy to use.* Navigation involves the links you place on each page connecting the user to other pages. A good site will let a user browse the site using three clicks or less to reach desired information. Navigation buttons should be direct. For example, "How do I place an order?", "I want to buy one now" and not just "Order form."

4. *Make ordering easy.* The order form will be discussed in the following sections. The golden rule is to make the order form as easy to use as

possible. At the same time, you need a seal of security certification to reassure the customer that their payment information is being kept safe.

5. *Give something away for free.* As we discussed before, you want to give something to the visitor for free. Your ultimate goal is to provide a free service on your web page that is so valuable to potential clients that they come back frequently to your site. For example, the seller of rare music LP records could post auction results for famous records each week. Collectors (very potential customers) would use the site to gain this valuable information. Your link to your catalog and order form would be part of each week's report. These potential customers are then just one click away from a sale.

6. *Use Meta tags.* These are read by the search engines to classify your site. More on this later.

In short, you want your pages to load fast, be obviously valuable to the potential customers, be well known on the internet, and invite purchases. At the same time you want a site different from anyone else's. That doesn't mean fancy graphics or novelties, although these can have a purpose. Instead, it usually means having information, a service, or a feature that is critically important to the potential customer.

For example, a lot of internet auction sites exist. However, the sites that offer industrial commodities direct to business and include information on how to set up every aspect of buying, selling, and moving the same commodities across national boarders are the most valuable sites. A purchasing agent may need steel, but a site that also provides instructions on the permits and paperwork needed to move it to Poland will get the repeat business. The information is actually more important to that purchasing agent than the steel. It saves him time, money, and effort—a lesson you should never forget when dealing with the internet.

Sales Force Automation

Another advantage for the web page is to have one to control your sales force. Such a page can be on a secured directory of your main site, or under a different domain name that is completely secured. Not only can you post schedules and appointments, you can have ready to download presentations and information files. In addition, you can link to a database at the company to show current inventory levels, prices, and delivery times. This allows the sales force to stay in the field and use their laptop computers to get the information and materials they need to make the sales calls. That results in more face-to-face time with customers.

When properly constructed and maintained, a good internet commerce site can outsell any other form of sales or marketing project ever conducted by a business.

The Catalog

The catalog is where you will list what you have for sell. It does not have to be called a catalog. In fact, it can take any of several forms. What is more important is that a potential customer can locate the item of interest very fast.

Unlike the printed catalog, the internet gives you the ability to provide rapid search capabilities. For example, you can have a list of product groups the user can click on to reach their intended area. Or, you can provide a search engine that will locate a specific item immediately.

One of the best approaches is to have a list of items with prices on a web page. Clicking any item brings up its description, terms, photos, and any other helpful information. On any page the user can click to order or place the item in a "shopping cart" for later review and purchase. (See www. amazon.com and www.ebay.com for excellent examples.)

In some businesses, such as consulting or financial advising, you need to provide a quote for each job. The catalog would list your capabilities and philosophy of client relationships. A single form would be presented to gather the information needed for preparing a quote. (See www.asr.9000.net and www.isogroup.simplenet.com/massquote.htm for examples.)

Doubtless you will eventually get into a situation where you need to tie a database to your website. That allows instant updating of catalog prices without the need to alter web pages and uploading them to the web site. Connecting databases to a web site is easy, but the details of making it "bullet-proof" and assuring complete accuracy is a subject in and of itself. Therefore, it is outside the scope of this book. You should consult experts in this field and any of the many books on this topic. Preferred database engines to use come from Oracle, Microsoft, and IBM.

The Order Form

All internet sales efforts have as their ultimate goal the task of steering potential customers to a point of ordering. The order form on the internet can be one of the most successful sales tools you have ever used, if it is used properly.

Any order form should be easy to understand and easy to use. Feel free to start by explaining how the form is to be filled out and what happens to the information. You need to reassure your internet audience that their information is secure. In addition, let them know up front how long it takes to fulfill an order.

You can also provide links to separate pages that explain your return policy, ordering policy, and complaint procedure. This should include the method used to cancel an order before shipping. Thus, each order will require a unique order number that is transmitted to the customer along with e-mail and 800 phone numbers they can use.

Be sure to clearly show your company's name, address, and phone numbers on pages used to sell products. This quietly assures the customer that your company is both professional and serious about staying in business.

Finally, there is information you can ask for from internet users without upsetting their level of comfort. Their name, address, phone number, and e-mail address are usually no problem. Personal information is what you want to avoid. This includes information such as their date of birth, sex, mother's maiden name, and the like. Credit card numbers are particularly sensitive and you should never ask for a Social Security number.

If you need payment information for a customer you must set up a secure web page. These are web pages presented from a special computer at the ISP or your location that encrypts any information being sent. You can make the user aware of this level of security by displaying the secure server certification on the web pages.

Alternatively, you can ask customers to phone or fax in orders forms with the purchasing information included. You always want to have an order form that can be printed from your web page, filled out by hand, and mailed with payment. This gives the really nervous customers a familiar alternative to use instead of ordering over the internet. See www.photo.9000.net for an example of how all of this is done.

The Hyperlink

We should also discuss the importance of the hyperlink. Of all of the inventions for the internet, this one is by far the most important. The web page allows anyone to post any information onto the internet. That is why it is said that the internet is slowly building up the sum knowledge of the human race. However, it is the hyperlink that makes that knowledge, no matter how obscurely hidden, just one mouse click away for an internet surfer.

As we discussed earlier, a web page can have a URL or web address. Any point on a page can also have a web address. The hyperlink enables the browser to jump from the link on one page to the associated address on another page. Let's look at how this works.

On your home page you describe the products you sell. In the description you mention your unique policy on customer service. The words *customer service* are underlined to indicate a link. When the user clicks on these words it will take him or her to the web address attached to this link. In this case the associated address is,

www.photo.9000.net/policy.htm

This is a page describing your customer service policy. The Back key on the internet browser can be pressed to return you to the home page at any time.

The real power of these links is that you can link to any place on the internet. For example, you may have a page of used equipment up for auction. The user clicks on an item and is taken to the item being auctioned at another site. In this way people visiting the auction site see your items and bid. At the same time, your regular viewers of your web page can also jump over to the auction house several thousand miles away, place a bid, and in one click be back to your web pages.

You could also make links to sites that provide further information in the field where you sell your product. In fact, a page of nothing but helpful links to other sites is usually quite popular on the internet and will bring in additional visitors. However, you do not put these types of links on your home page. That only encourages first-time visitors to leave your page before they learn more about you and your services.

More Powerful Tools for Web Pages

Web addresses

Let's look at how the address works and how you use such addresses for smart selling. HTTP or Hypertext Transfer Protocol is a method developed for linking a user to a particular web site. This ability to link is something we will discuss in following sections. Thus, http:// calls up the method of linking. "WWW" stands for the world wide web. "Voyager" is the name of the company you are contacting, it is also known as the domain name. "Net" means that this is a network site. The more familiar ".com" represents a commercial site.

As mentioned in the section on e-mail, if you choose your domain name carefully you can make navigation to your product and ordering information easier for your potential clients. Take the case of the Lexus automotive company. Obviously, you take the domain name "lexus.com." However, for smart selling you also take the following domain names.

> lexus-usa.com
> lexusdealers.com
> LS400.com
> GS400.com
> ES300.com
> RX300.com
> LX 470.com

and so on. These are the names of your primary products and your alternative company names. All of these domain names can be "pointed" to the same web site or used for different types of sales strategies on their own. Each would land on a unique page that matches the product or company. This way, a potential customer that doesn't quite know how to find your site might punch in a best guess for your location on the internet. With several possibilities covered they are more likely to find your site without frustration. In addition, once they find the car they like they can lock onto the domain name of the car and go right to the information they want. In addition, the multiple names will increase your chances of landing a top spot on a search engine. If your product line has a recognizable character associated with your sales literature, you can also registered that as a domain name. For example, "Dilbert.com."

Links

Links can take other forms. For example, you can create a file download link. If you sell a product where software is involved and your customers need frequent updates or enhancements, this is a very powerful tool. You can post an announcement of the newest bit of software for your product and link it to an FTP download. When the user clicks on the link the software is automatically downloaded to their computer.

Another powerful tool is the mail link. In your sales presentation on the internet you can sprinkle your web site with the message . . .

> "Of course, if you have any questions, just drop me a line *via* e-mail."

When clicked, this link will open a program at the users' end to compose and send an e-mail directly to your e-mail address. If you keep the internet close at hand, you can respond quickly to these initial requests for further information. Giving the impression that answers are always nearby and personalized at your site makes you very competitive.

Search engines

Search engines track and list web pages on the internet. In return, they offer anyone a quick way to look up sites by topic, style, or name. Sites like www.yahoo.com, www.ask.com, and www.hotbot.com are all excellent examples of search engines. You can search in any one of several ways. You can enter keywords, look through categories, or select specific topics highlighted on the home page.

Search engines find web sites to list in one of two basic ways. One is to "spider" the web. That is, a web agent program searches the net for new sites. Once found, a new site is examined by title, meta tags, and text content of the home page. The program then assigns keywords to the site. The second method is to have the web author submit the new site for listing.

Here, typically, the author describes the web site using forms available on the search engine.

Getting Discovered on the Internet

A critical point is reached when your web site is finished and ready for presentation. Now you have to inform the world that your site exists and encourage visitors to come by for a look. Here are the techniques, from most effective to least, for making your site known.

- Search engines
- e-mail announcements
- link from other web sites
- word of mouth
- magazine and TV ads
- article in a periodical mentioning your site or about your site
- catalogs
- newspaper, radio, or mail ads
- banner ads on the internet

Notice that some of these techniques you can control and some you cannot. The search engine strategy is where over half of the internet users go to find a site. Search engines list and classify web sites by topics. An internet user enters a search request and a list of potentially matching web sites appears. Your job is to make you site appear at the top of these lists.

To try out some of the most popular search engines, browse any of the following:

www.yahoo.com
www.excite.com
www.hotbot.com
www.lycos.com
www.ask.com

Let's take a specific example of how to manually place your site on a search engine. At Yahoo, you need to select a category that best describes your product or service. For example, a photo shop site would go to an area such as business/photography/retailers. At the bottom of the page presented by Yahoo is a small link for suggesting a new site. You click on this and answer the information requested on a series of forms. This only starts the process. The Meta tags on your site and how the page is layed out will also determine where you get located. Services are available to teach you how to build proper meta tags and to help get your site to the top of search engine lists. Consult the internet for the most popular methods currently being used. See the following sites:

- vancouver-webpages.com/META/mk-metas.html
- free.elch.net/meta.shtml
- www.softseek.com/Internet/Web_Publishing_Tools/HTML_META_Tag_Tools/
- www.siteowner.com

Once the visitors arrive at your site you have a precious few seconds to convince them to stay and a few minutes to make repeat visitors out of them. It is the repeat customers that tend to place the most orders. The features of a web page that keeps visitors coming back are, in order of effectiveness:

- high quality and useful content
- ease of use
- quick loading and downloading times
- updated frequently
- incentives like discounts and coupons
- favorite brands
- cutting edge technology
- games
- purchasing capabilities
- content that can be customized
- chat rooms
- desktop publishing quality of the site

Note how having the most attractive site is not nearly as important as having a site that is helpful to the potential customer and easy to use. Your customers are in a hurry looking for things on the internet that can solve their problems. Present a solution quickly and you have a repeat customer.

Creating an Order Form

Let's take a look at a well developed order form and see what makes it work well.

"Welcome to our order form. We can provide various forms of *shipping* for your order. We accept Visa, MasterCard, American Express, and checks. Be sure to read why your ordering information is *secure*. We offer a 30-day money back *return policy*.

Your Name: _____

E-mail address: _____

Item you are interested in: _____ Number you would like: _____

How will you be paying: _____ "

Notice how the form has a few opening links before the form is reached. These direct the user of the form to further instructions, policies, and more information about the items to be ordered and the preferred method of shipment. In this way, a first-time user can be well-informed before using the form. An experienced user can quickly move on to making the purchase.

Working within the web page software you select the check boxes, buttons, scrolling text boxes, and drop down lists you wish to use. The idea is to make a simple, easy to use, and appealing to look at order form. When a customer submits this first form the information provided is used to select the next form they will see.

For example, credit card customers will go to a secure web site and enter charge card information. After that all customers are directed to the page that asks where the products should be shipped. The bill is calculated and presented for final approval. The key is to keep the process as easy and short as possible.

As before, use direct and simple language for the navigation button to the order page, such as "sign me up," "sounds good, I'll take one," "place on order," and so forth.

The actual order form will either be a direct order or a request for a quote. In both cases their are types of information you can ask for without offending most internet users. This includes:

- their name
- company name
- address
- phone number
- e-mail account
- how they would like to pay for the products

Items to avoid where possible include:

- mother's maiden name
- sex of customer
- age of customer or birth date
- credit card numbers
- typical demographic data (such as hobbies, income, neighborhood, job, etc.)

Personal information is given very reluctantly on the internet. If you need personal or demographic information, use mailed follow-up literature to attempt obtaining these data. For credit card numbers, be sure the customer is sent to a separate form emblazoned with security certificates to make it clear that "snoopers" and "hackers" will not get their information.

Order forms also should be as short as possible, have a simple layout, and contain clear instructions. The instructions on how to fill out the form should be tested by letting a small group of people try figuring out the form in a test. You should quickly discover if you have badly worded requests or missing advice. You should also be ready to modify your form when you discover that some people fill out the form incorrectly for the same reason.

For example, you may have designed a form with two lines for a street address. You intended for customers to put the street address on line one and any suite, apartment, or other information on the second line. Instead, you see people consistently putting their city in the second box. Clearly they are not looking ahead when filling out the form. You need to redesign the form to eliminate this problem.

Another good feature is to have quick names for regular customers. This is where the customer selects a unique name for themselves, like "camera-guy," and a password. When they enter these at your site the order form automatically fills in their address and payment information.

Study the order forms at amazon.com and ebay.com to see how it is done well. These types of powerful ordering forms should either be designed by a specialist or purchased from one of the software packages designed for electronic commerce.

The simple forms work best. Short, easy-to-use forms invite customers to place a quick order. Catalogs that allow people to check off the quantities and types they need are popular. So too are the "shopping cart" systems where selected items are placed in a temporary database for the customer to review and alter before the point of purchase.

Once the form is completed by a customer, one of several things can be set up to happen next. Some systems automatically check credit card numbers and addresses to verify within seconds whether this is a valid order. You can have the order e-mailed directly to you for review and approval. You can have the valid orders e-mailed automatically to a warehouse and fulfillment operation. A database can record the order and compile a series of product orders to many vendors based on the total requests for the day. Copies of requests for quotes can be sent to field agents around the world for comment or completion.

In short, you can automate the forms to speed the purchasing and fulfillment process. This includes depositing the money, confirming the shipment to the customer, automatically sending a thank-you e-mail, and getting a report on all this activity sent directly to you, no matter where you are in the world.

Once completed, you post the test form to a hidden web page for testing. Try filling it out in several ways and make sure the information is being collected and sent reliably and as expected. Once you are satisfied with the final order forms, then open them to the public.

Contact Management Software

Of critical importance to making yourself effective on the internet, and in real life, is the use of contact management software. These are the programs that record with whom you have talked, sent information, met with, made pitches, and have closed past sales. In short, every potential and real customer you have had any type of contact. However, as IS manager, you will need to coordinate which package is used in your company and which parts of the package will be attached with which portions of your internet presence.

The software then keeps you informed of who you promised to call today, when the next critical pitch is being made, the name of the spouse and children of your best customers, and a host of other information that helps you to build customer relationships. Some of these programs can even be used to send personalized letters to existing customers on important dates or anniversaries. The type of software you use for internet sales can be your current program, or a new one, as long as it has a few additional features.

1. You should be able to link your e-mail messages, both coming and going, to your contact management software records.

2. Regularly scheduled announcements set up by the contact management software should be capable of being sent by e-mail.

3. You will want to be able to list the web sites you have visited for later reference. Good packages will let you make a copy of competing sites for your reference.

4. Your calendar should be downloadable in a way that can be posted to a sales force-wide calendar on the internet. This is optional, but is a very powerful tool when used well. It lets your sales force stay in the field much longer than normal while the sales manager can be very mobile at the same time.

5. The best package will link to other computer applications and let you automate routine tasks. For example, you can fully automate both e-mail and real mail responses to potential and existing customers using personal data from your files to make it look like you are paying full attention to each customer.

Using Your Software

The best approach to using contact management software with your internet activities is to have sales and customer relations staff launch the program and leave it running all the time. Then, when they read through e-mail or visit customer web sites they can jump to the contact management screen to make notes or link messages. They can also make notes to contact specific people at particular times. Let's look at some examples of this.

The sales manager with a sales force of ten field representatives receives the promotional literature for a new product. He uses this to prepare a basic PowerPoint presentation for the new product. This, in turn, is e-mailed to the 10 sales representatives in the field. The manager's contact software records this with alerts to check back and make sure everyone got the material.

After two weeks, an automatic message is sent to the sales force asking for reactions from customers on the new product. The reply e-mails are collected together and summarized to help revise sales forecasts.

Bill is reading through e-mail one day when he notices a mention of a new government contract bid being issued for office furniture. He is not the government sales representative for the office furniture company he represents, that is Sally Tally's job. He sends a copy of the e-mail to Sally with a note to point out the opportunity.

Now Bill goes to his contact management software and sets a to-do alarm to check Monday with Sally. He also attaches the original e-mail to this note. Then he makes a second to-do (no alarm) to draft a quick proposal that he and Sally work together on this sale. Chances are Sally will have little interest in sharing the success with anyone. But, Bill now has the original e-mail and his documented offer to help to show his boss that he started the process that led to a new account.

Ed is reading through his e-mail and finding several people requesting the free demo CD-ROM his client company is offering in a mail campaign. The potential customer's name, company, address, and e-mail address is copied from the e-mails right into Ed's contact management software. Microsoft Word is automatically booted up to a prepared response letter. The potential customer's name and address is added to the letter and it is mailed out with a disk. A confirming e-mail message is sent thanking the potential customer for the request and informing them that the disk is on its way 2nd day air. Another e-mail with the basic shipping information is used to generate the label that Ed's office assistant uses to ship out the package. In three days, Ed's contact software will let him know it is time to contact these people and ask if the disk got there OK.

As you can see, contact management software helps the sales people to keep their contact and related information straight. It helps remind them when it is time to do something in the sales process. It also automates many of their tasks. The result is that they can handle 10 times more customers or more at a time. This is important on the internet where traffic can get very large, very fast. Therefore, as IS manager, you have to design and implement this system to make it "bomb-proof" from failures. You also have to train people on how to use it effectively. Finally, you have to perform frequent back-ups.

Discussion Groups

Great community-building devices are the discussion group and the chat room. A chat room is where people at one web site can type in messages to each other in real time. All visitor's to that site can view the messages and participate, if they wish. A discussion group, in contrast, allows people to post messages on a particular topic. A visitor can respond to any posted message at any time. As such, the replies may build up over a period of days or weeks.

Either way, these devices encourage your customers to talk to each other. How often have you been in a store and wanted to talk to somebody that actually uses the product you are considering buying? On the internet, with a discussion group available, you can instantly tune into hundreds of users from around the world and read their thoughts and opinions. By providing this service you make your site more valuable and show the confidence you have in your product.

Auction Sites

Auction sites are web sites that allow you to place items up for bid. This gives you several advantages. You can escape the retail price structure, get rid of unwanted inventory, and promote the active participation of your customers. If your web site links to an auction site where you regularly put your products or services up for auction, you encourage your potential customers to visit your site frequently.

Auction sites are also very powerful areas on the internet. Some retail businesses have closed shop and moved all activity to an auction site like Ebay. Auction sites give you access to a worldwide audience of eager buyers. New industrial auction sites give you direct access to the purchasing managers of corporations. This gives you the potential of selling products 24 hours a day across a whole new range of items.

Managed Mail Lists

Another powerful internet sales tool is the managed mail list. This is software that allows you to build up a huge list of e-mail addresses and post messages to the list with one e-mail. People join the list by sending an e-mail request to subscribe. The signing up and maintenance of the list is all automatic, requiring very little of your time.

By having a large list of existing customers or people interested in your products, you have the ability to quickly send notifications of special offers, updates, or new products. You can also use the list to send a monthly newsletter or quarterly catalog. This will help your customer to feel unique while creating a new audience for your product.

If you can offer extremely important information, it is possible to charge for being on the list. Or, you could form an "A-list" of the key people in your industry and restrict your mailing to that list. Only "special" customers are allowed on the list. This can be a real marketing advantage.

Streaming Audio/Video

The internet allows streaming audio and video, where people can listen to music and voices, or watch video. This can add sound and movement to your sales presentation. It can help demonstrate your product or service. You can also teach, inform, and announce using these tools. However, it has to be used carefully because it consumes much of the bandwidth of your communication with the internet.

The Supporting Sales Tools

These are just some of the communications tools the internet offers. To make them work effectively as sales tools you need some other tools that support these means of communication. As IS manager, you are going to be asked to set up and distribute these tools. Be ready to respond on how many of these resources can be effectively established and distributed at any one time. You need to keep the introduction of such tools to a minimum that still accomplishes the company's sales goals. At the same time you have to prevent the overwhelming of your own staff.

Your company will need to track both customer and potential customers. You need to control internet traffic and manage your own time. You will also need to coordinate customer requests with follow-up activities.

Cell phones

Most sales representatives have to travel. Cell phones are a great way to always be in touch with the office. They can also be used to download e-mail. Thus, you can always stay on top of internet customers. Some sales professionals have just one phone number that rings both the office and cell phone. This gives them a high degree of mobility while also being constantly available for customers. However, a company needs a cell phone policy on who gets the phones and how they are to be used. Because they are so portable, you will need to track their distribution carefully. This will include a rapid reaction plan when one is lost or stolen.

PDAs

Personal digital assistants (or PDAs) like the Palm Pilot are mobile versions of your contact software and internet access. They can coordinate schedules with your contact management software while having a modem that can dial into the internet. By downloading your electronic sales brochures and price lists in a PDA you can respond to customer requests from any location with a phone. Again, you will need to control their distribution.

Laptops

When the sales staff needs complete computing power in a highly mobile form, the laptop computer is used. This allows them to take your office anywhere, including back to their homes. With all sales information loaded in the hard drive they can prepare quotes, faxes, e-mails, and presentations anywhere. They can even make face-to-face presentations using a laptop.

The internet the sales force can check e-mail, update your web site, prepare a managed mail list postings, or any of the other internet sales activities we have discussed. The new wired sales representative that is always on the road now hires a driver and spends travel time working on the laptop. However, the laptop can contain valuable information about your company, so encryption and anti-theft methods must be in place.

Fax sites

The internet sales approach is best when it is supported by non-internet alternatives. By giving your customers several ways to contact your company to place an order you are making the customer more comfortable. For example, a fax site at your office can be used to provide 24-hour services, such as fax-on-demand where a person calls in and presses a key to be promptly faxed your current price list.

Voice mail

Toll free numbers to real sales people gives internet customers uncomfortable with buying over the internet a friendly person they can work with to complete the sale. Voice mail makes sure that any person calling at any time gets the call answered. Voice mail has to be carefully designed to make self-ordering very easy and to make it very clear that each message will be answered very soon. The soon to be introduced voice-over-IP technologies will make it possible for customers to place "calls" from their computer to your company. Please note how this type of technology ropes in the IS manager to implementing and controlling the new system.

Other possibilities

There are other support technologies that are available, such as flexible working hours for your staff, having staff in a different time zones to cover the off-hours communications, and the like. What your company uses will depend on its particular situation and needs. The best rule of thumb is to use the minimal number of internet communication tools and support tools that will accomplish your sales goals.

Getting Noticed on the Internet Is Critical

It is estimated that more than three million companies now conduct business on the internet to an audience soon to reach one billion. No matter what business you are in, chances are that some of your competitors are already on the internet. Your job is to find a way to distinguish yourself from these competitors and drive customers to your site.

The best opening strategy is to analyze the competitors and find ways to beat them at their own game. This is where you conduct a thorough search of the internet for anyone selling what you sell. Study their sites and look at how they present themselves. You need to determine the following:

1. Where are they strong.
2. Where are they weak.
3. How easy was it to find their site?
4. Do we want to work with or against this group?
5. Which meta tags are used on their site?

Competitive information will provide you with the intelligence you need to steer your e-commerce site into a competitive position. Once there you compete strongly for the available customers.

Key to being competitive is to get your web site to the top of the search engine lists. This is accomplished by listing your new web site at the major search engine sites. There are services on the internet that will do this for you automatically for free or a slight charge. Avoid these at all costs. This is how the majority of sites get listed. Your site will end up at the bottom of most lists this way.

Instead, either hire a professional web promoter or do it yourself. The way to get to the top of the lists is to go to each search engine and personally enter the needed information. For example, in Yahoo! you find the category that best matches your web site and click the "Add URL" button at the bottom of the page. A three-part form takes you through the process.

You also incorporate Meta tags on your web page. These are hidden data sets that describe your web site using keywords. The search engines will typically scan your web site and categorize it automatically. Meta tags leave very specific information on how it is to be listed. You can see the meta tags at other sites by viewing a web page and clicking on View, Source in your browser. The meta tags are clearly marked at the top of a page.

Let's look at a quick example. You are setting up the web site for a law office that wants to get clients from the internet. The keywords you enter at the search engines and the Meta tags contain items such as:

- law
- lawyers
- attorneys
- divorce
- civil law
- free advice
- problem solving

Notice how the terms are selected not only to describe the type of practice being offered, but are spread out over possibilities to pull in more searches than a typical law office description might obtain. That is, a person facing divorce may have a personal problem to solve and will enter "problem solving" as a search term in a search engine. She then sees a law firm saying that it can help solve your problems related to divorce. This gets her curious enough to look at the site because the discovery was unexpected.

After that you spread the word to other sites. The best way to do this is to visit the non-competing sites that would normally refer traffic to a site like yours. The law firm shown above would approach the various bar associations. A commodity broker would go to import/export sites. Many sales sites want to be associated with the search engines themselves.

Once at the related sites (the ones with a lot of internet traffic), you make inquiries about being linked. Linking is when the large site adds you to their list of recommended links to other important sites. Link pages are immensely popular on the internet. Getting on a large site's link list will bring a considerable flow of traffic to your site.

The usual addition of your web site address in all correspondence and literature will help to make even more people aware of your site. The idea is to make it easy for anyone to find your site. That means you have to check every few months to make sure your company's web site is still at the top of most lists.

Finally, you can always pay to gain a position on a search engine. This can be as a shopping site on a popular service like Yahoo or American Online. It can also be a featured link on a topic page. Or, it could be an advertisement on a portal site. Either way, money will buy you positioning. You have to balance the positioning against costs and number of potential customers that will be drawn to your site.

Build a Community or Use an Existing Community

Once you have a strategic internet sales plan, a web site, and a marketing niche selected you are ready to begin. Take notes on your sales objectives, list these objectives, match the appropriate internet tools for each objective. Boil this list down to the minimum number of tools you will need. Formulate where you want to start your internet activities by either building a community or latching onto an existing community.

Examine what your competitors are doing on the internet. What do your customers need that these competing sites are not delivering? Where are they weak? Exploit these weaknesses. Your main objective is to build a community of potential customers. How is that done?

Foundations

Communities can be built around foundations laid down with:

- newsletters
- updating services

- discussion groups
- index and link services
- managed mail lists
- auction sites
- online education
- professional networking

and other techniques. Find the one that best fulfills the missing information or service that your potential customers need.

Famous communities on the internet

At this point we should take a few moments to discuss what a community looks like and how it functions to draw in regular visitors. To do this we should examine a few famous internet sites.

The first example is the auction site eBay. In a typical month, eBay's home page will receive over 1.5 billion hits. Over two million items are up for bid on a typical day. The impact of this one site has been massive on the internet and the real world. The prices set on eBay have established the value of many objects. For example, cameras auctioned on eBay have set the real value of a used camera, even more than the standard blue books developed for pricing used photographic equipment. Retail shops have closed their doors and moved all operations to eBay. This is especially true of computer sales.

Therefore we need to look at the eBay home page to see why the site works so well. For one thing, it is easy to navigate and understand. A level of trust is established in the site due to its use of certified security systems and a clear set of rules that protects both buyers and sellers.

Please note the following features of eBay in Figure S2–1.

A) The largest feature on the home page is the four most likely first requests by a new visitor, how does this work, where do I sign up, and so on.

B) Surrounding these links are examples of the auctions that await the visitor. These tease a new visitor into staying at the site to see what people are selling.

Figure S2-1. Example of a Community Web Site

C) A search box is provided to allow visitors to look for a specific item.

D) A café creates a community center where bidders and new users can meet to chat about auctioning or to ask questions, or to post requests for an item that cannot be found.

We can see that eBay uses the rules we just stated. They know their audience's needs and expectations. Navigation is easy. They provide a free service (searching through items for pricing). Visitors are encouraged to linger and talk to other bidders. Bidders can ask sellers questions through e-mail. In other words, the environment of an auction is nicely simulated. At the same time the unique nature of the internet makes the experience of eBay fit internet expectations. Here is an auction bigger than anything in the real world. Unlike a real auction you can instantly find the owner of the item for sale and ask questions. The thrill of bidding against others in real time is preserved.

Figure S2-2. CNN's Financial Network Web Page

Actual Broadcast information

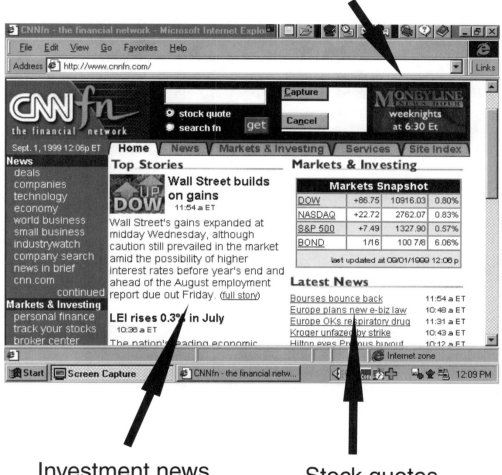

Investment news

Stock quotes

In short, eBay represents a big success story on the internet. And this success was no accident. A careful sales and marketing plan for the site was used and the web site designed for the expectations of the audience.

Another example of a community on the internet is the CNNfn web site. They too receive millions of hits per day. The audience for this site are the stock market investors of the world. CNN runs a separate cable channel for financial news. One would normally expect the supporting web site to emphasize coming programs. Instead, the needs of the customers come first.

The site includes breaking investment news, stock quotes live, and alert services. Research and other investment tools are made available for free. The reputation of CNN is used along with the availability of free services to make this site a community. Many investors bookmark this site for frequent checks on the day's news and investment activities (see Figure S2–2).

The third example is Yahoo! This is a very well known site on the internet (see Figure S2–3). It's success came from providing a service, for free, that formally wasn't on the internet—searching for web sites. The search engine feature of Yahoo has expanded to include categories, special interest areas, and customized reports. At the same time, Yahoo is pursuing a strategy

Figure S2-3. Yahoo Home Web Page

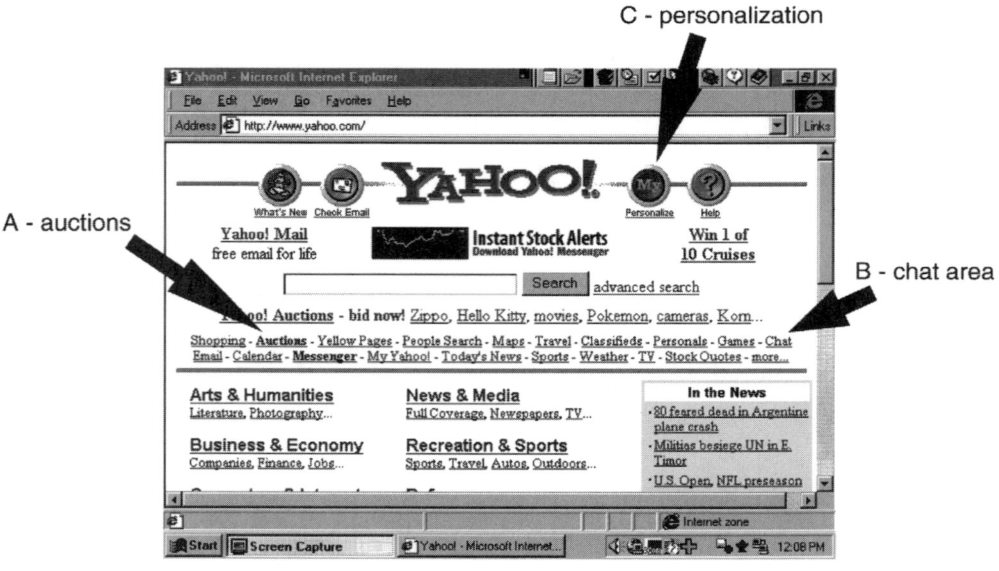

of making the site more of a community by adding chat areas, auctions, and other community building technologies.

As you can see from the Yahoo home page, there are several community building tactics being used.

A—auctions

B—chat areas

C—personalized services

Finally, we want to examine a small community on the internet. This one is the Pentax site. Here we find a lot of what you would expect from a web site supporting optical and photographic equipment (see Figure S2–4). Product lines and features are dominating the site. However, a unique

Figure S2-4. Pentax Web Site Home Page

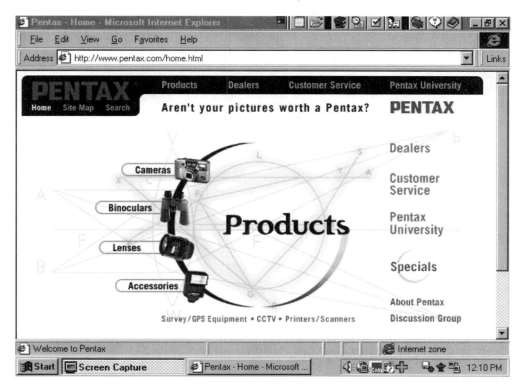

Figure S2–5. Pentax Discussion Board

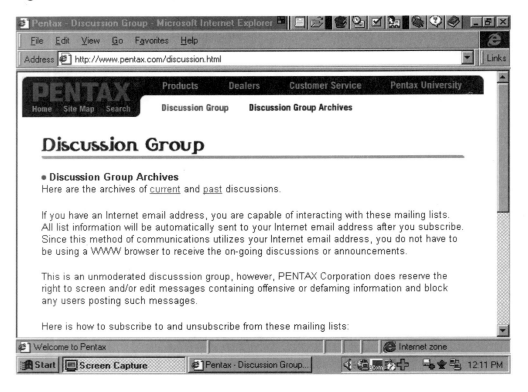

customer discussion board is also provided as a community building tool (see Figure S2–5).

What this does is give the consumer the ability to not only learn about the various cameras and how people are using them, but to ask questions of current owners of the equipment. It is not unusual to find blunt questions such as "Is the ZX-5 any good?" being asked and answered.

Casting Nets to Draw in Visitors

Once you have your foundation laid, you need to draw internet visitors to your site. This is done by aggressively listing your site on the search engines, making e-mail announcements, and posting site information on all printed literature and advertisement material. You can also send press releases. However, a good amount of time should be spent asking related internet sites to link to your site.

What you are doing is casting a wide net to gather in interested people to your site. If properly planned and designed, your site will make these visitors linger and come back for repeat visits. This allows the traditional sales model to progress. Now that you have an audience you can start building a relationship and making presentations.

Is the Plan Working?

How will you know if your plan is working? The best way to do this is to track the internet activity you experience and make some comparisons to other methods of selling your product. For example, the number of referrals or requests for quotes you get from the internet versus those from your toll-free phone number.

Other measures include the amount of repeat business, effectiveness of sales presentations, the efficiency (or amount of money needed) to close a sale, the average time from first contact to closing of a sale, and pure sales volume. These are all good ways to measure success. The number of people visiting your web site (also called page hits) is not a good measure because it is not correlated with successful sales.

Once you discover an internet approach that is successful, effective, and efficient, you pour more resources into development. For example, if you find that your managed mail list promotions get three times the volume of customers than any other sales method, internet or not, you should focus more attention on making a larger and better list.

Force Multiplication—Force Multiply Wherever You Can

When you wish to go beyond a strong internet presence, you look into the concept of force-multiplication. This technique involves finding a tool, technique, or tactic that increases your sales effectiveness by orders of magnitude.

In other words, sales don't go up 10%, 20% or 30%—they increase 100%, 200%, or 300%.

Luckily, the internet is an excellent environment for discovery or use of force-multiplication tools. The network is so young and flexible that new methods of greatly increasing effectiveness are being found almost every day. For example, a search engine that can guide you to any one of millions of web sites is a good example of force-multiplication. Developed by only a few people, they serve millions and have generated billions of dollars in revenue.

The first multipliers you will discover are the managed mail lists and discussion groups. Just one person can dominate a subject area by providing timely information to thousands of people. Once attracted into a community, the sales professional can make presentations to this "captured" audience.

The internet is also filled with millions of people requesting specific types of information. By consulting the e-mail advertising lists, where people have asked for sales information on specific products, you can generate thousands of leads within a day. Effective use of e-mail can create sales volumes per sales professional much higher than possible by any other media.

To accomplish this you need a good plan and knowledge of what your audience is looking to buy. For example, check out www.isogroup. simplenet.com. This is a simple site that provides free information to companies trying to get ISO 9000 registered. One step in the process is the hiring of a third party, called a registrar, to perform the registration audit. One of the links at this site takes the visitor to a page where filling out one form will result in up to 15 quotes from various registrars.

This is a clever use of the internet. The companies would normally spend weeks contacting various registrars, filling out their forms, and waiting for quotes. This service at the isogroup page cuts the effort down to one form and the response time down to a couple of days. The user of this service benefits from time savings, the registrars get new potential customers, and the isogroup gets a fee for each successful contract that results. Everyone wins. Because the transmission of the requests for quotes is nearly automatic, the effort involved is minimal, yet hundreds of potential clients can be handled by a person working just an hour or two a week on this service.

In your situation, you need to find the right mix of service, product, and people to get a similar result. For example, you can use your sales staff "in depth." This is where one person receives all e-mail inquiries and assigns them to particular staff people. Standard questions are answered with pre-pared answers. Each staff person then follows-up with the inquiries until a sale is made or the lead grows cold. When properly designed, such coordinated efforts can let a few people handle thousands of customers each month. It can also allow you to close more sales per inquiry.

Another approach

Another force-multiplication tool is to create new products based on your internet activities. For example, your discussion group used to build a community of customers may contain a lot of useful advice. By boiling this down into a newsletter or CD-ROM update service, you have a new product that can be sold. The content is created by your own customers. You resell their stories, advice, or knowledge back to the general community.

Final Step—Conquering Internet Territory

The final goal in any strategic sales plan should be the expansion of markets, increased sales, new customers, in short the conquest of new sales territory. The internet is no different in this regard from the real world. The only real difference is that internet territory remains largely up for grabs.

Think of the internet as a large, mostly unexplored land where distant interest groups from overseas are sending in explorers. Most of the current internet sales presence is Lewis and Clark sort of stuff where a couple of people are carving out trading posts. Most major commerce sites on the internet were started by five or fewer people.

Now think what would happen in such a land if someone sent in an organized army to conquer the territory. There would be little or no resistance and no limit on conquest. This is the opportunity awaiting the aggressive sales force on the internet.

This type of strategic approach relies on the following approach we have discussed before.

1. Knowing the competition.
2. Attacking where you are strong.
3. Attacking where the competitors are weak.

4. Taking advantage of any opportunities you discover.

5. Having a coordinated plan.

6. Being flexible enough to change plans as your strategy unfolds.

Needless to say this is a topic worthy of considerable discussion. For right now we will merely discuss the high points and suggest that you spend more time on this topic once you have established yourself firmly on the internet.

Knowing the Competition

Just like any great commander, it pays to know your competition well. The internet provides many opportunities to learn a lot about your competitors. For example, it is extremely likely that your competitor also has a Web site. Therefore, your first stop is to visit that Web site.

Begin by going to a popular search engine and entering the name of your competitor. Also try some keywords for the type of business people are in. Make notes on how high on the search list your site and your competitor's site land. Then visit competing sites and take note of what makes it attractive and where it has weaknesses.

Also take the time to examine the other Web sites that came up in your search list. Examine these other sites to see if any of them are different from your site. Watch for the same rules we have taught you earlier. Do the competing sites offer something to the customer for free? Is there helpful information on any of these sites you cannot get anywhere else? Are they promoting a community of potential customers?

The idea is to find where your competitors are weak and to exploit those weaknesses. You also want to take advantage of any opportunities that are presented. For example, if no one is leading a discussion group on a topic related to your product, this is a good time to start one.

Attacking where you are strong

Earlier, we talked about the importance of knowing where your company and its product is strong. That strength must be used as your primary means of competitive contact. Take the example of the investment house that has a world famous stockbroker on its staff. This stockbroker's advice is greatly admired and followed in the trading community. This is a strength. You exploit this strength by giving the internet community access to his opinions for free. Soon a large number of potential and current customers cluster around this advice.

This could take the form of a daily newsletter the stockbroker publishes only on the internet. This will cast a very large net over the community of internet users and funnel interested investors to this one site. From there you can make your presentation for the services the investment house offers.

Attacking where the competitors are weak

At the same time you must attack the competitors where they are weak. Once a competitor is off-balance, it takes considerable effort for them to be able to compete back against you. For example, an ISO 9000 registrar discovered that all the other registrars were very hesitant to discuss the price of their services. This is a weakness to be exploited. The registrar then posted examples of the cost of registration services recently performed along with information on the size and type of company involved. They also offered a free no obligation quote for registration services with a promise that a sales representative would not pester them to sign a contract.

What they discovered was that the page giving examples of the prices paid for registration services was being visited more than any other page on their Web site. This confirmed that customers wanted to know price information. By providing this, they again focused potential customers to their Web site.

Taking advantage of any opportunities you discover

Sometimes you'll discover an opportunity that can be seized on the internet. For example, you may find out that your customers tend to use a specific discussion area. By visiting web sites and monitoring the conversation you are able to distinguish their real needs.

Take the situation where purchasing agents from many companies are at a conference discussing the frustration of trying to find the proper export papers for several emerging industrialized countries. Overhearing the conversation was the sales representative of a major rolled steel company. Going back to his company he redesigned the Web site to include links to import-export assistance sites and a library of standard export forms. Sales increased exponentially.

Having a coordinated plan

It is not enough to merely compete on the internet. Instead, you need to have a strategic plan for competition that is well coordinated with all of your resources. For instance, if your company has several sales representatives they can break up the task of examining competing sites among the individuals. Marketing initiatives can then be coordinated with other departments in your company. You have to make sure that the single message you are sending out to the internet about the value of your product is being repeated by everyone on your team.

Then there is the issue of time. The timing of your response to your audience on the internet and where you choose to respond must also be coordinated. Depending upon the particular situation this can take varying amounts of effort and time to plan, coordinate, and implement.

Being flexible enough to change plans as your strategy unfolds

No matter how well you plan your competitive strategy, things can go wrong. A major mistake can be committed, a new opportunity spotted, or a new competitor might suddenly appear. Therefore, you need to keep your plan flexible so that last-minute changes can be made in reaction to any changes in your competitive environment.

For example, you may have just signed the deal to have your Web site featured on a nationally known Web site. Just after your site first appears, you discover your partner has been bought out by a larger corporation. You'll have to act quickly to make sure that the promotion of the national site is preserved.

Or, perhaps, one of your competitors may introduce free training modules for its customers. Your team believes that this is a competitive advantage for the other side. You need to move quickly to decide how, when, and where you will respond.

The end goal of your efforts is to seize territory on the internet. However, you may remember from earlier conversations that the internet does not really have time or space. This makes it extremely difficult to establish boundaries. Therefore, you are seeking a different type of territory. You want to find the audience of potential customers and command their eye balls to watch your internet information more often than anyone else's.

You will also want to convert as many potential customers into paying customers as possible. This includes increasing the amount of money such people are willing to spend on the internet. These goals can be compatible with your strategy capture territory. Specifically, you can capture the audience of other Web sites for your own use.

One example of those are sites where users can fill out a request for quote. Then several competing firms receive the information and issue quotes. If you are the site that setup such a quoting service you now dominate the bidding field. This gives you a considerable advantage. Not only are you quoting the common customers you would regularly see, but you now have requests coming from the customers of competitors. If you are the first to offer such a service you tend to shut out the possibility of competing services being set up. As you can quickly see, you can go a long way beyond the simple points made here. You are limited only by your imagination for what you can accomplish on the internet.

Now It's Your Turn

It is time to put what you have learned to work for you. Work through the following steps by yourself and then with your sales team. See what idea you generate for using the internet effectively. The only rule is that there are no rules.

1. What is your primary product or service?
2. Who currently forms the base of your customers?
3. Which groups should be using your product but for some reason are not fully aware of your product?
4. Now, visit the sites of your competitors. Where are they strong? Where are they weak or repeating the same message?
5. Perform an internet search on keywords related to your product. What did you discover by visiting these sites?
6. What discussion groups address topics related to your product?
7. Put all of this information together and brainstorm ways to make your internet presence strong. Also think of ways of capturing the audience for your product.

Summary

As we have seen from the discussion in this chapter, the internet has a huge potential for any organization willing to use effective and efficient sales and marketing methods. However, to use those methods you have to be keenly aware of the particular preferences and expectations of the internet audience.

Too much time is being spent on developing powerful and glossy e-commerce sites without a proportionate amount of effort forming and co-ordinating a sales plan of attack. Several of our tests have shown that a determined sales force on the internet can take advantage of the lack of serious, large-scale marketing efforts by large corporations that would normally dominate a medium.

Final points

Before we conclude our report we want to emphasize the following points.

- Everything has to be carefully planned and coordinated.
- Don't quit trying after the first "success" on the internet—keep growing and learning.
- Cast a wide net for new visitors for your web site—the more the better.
- Make all visitors to your site feel welcomed through personal e-mail and by giving away something for free.
- Always follow professional sales practices based on the traditional sales model—people respect the open, honest, and professional sales representative.
- Keep your contact software and e-mail programs running on a computer at all times.
- Work the promotions of the web site all of the time.
- Use cell phones, laptop computers, and other tools to keep the internet near you.
- Stay flexible—the internet changes constantly and you must be ready to exploit fleeting opportunities.

Suggested Web Sites to Investigate

e-business magazines on the web

www.netmarketmakers.com—Net marketing magazine

www.sellitontheweb.com—General sales on the web magazine

www.ecommercetimes.com—Huge e-commerce magazine

discussion groups (newsgroups)

alt.ecommerce

alt.internet.ecommerce

e-commerce sites

www.zdnet.com/enterprise/e-business—Ziff-Davis site on e-commerce with 10 best and worst of the net

www.ecommerce.internet.com—huge site

www.strikeitrich.com—Jaclyn Easton's site on successful business web sites

www.studioarchetype.com/cheskin—e-commerce trust study

www.emarketer.com—marketing on the internet site

www.gbd.org—global business dialogue on e-commerce

www.globeset.com/Commerce—e-commerce professionals' site

www.intermktgrp.com—briefings on e-commerce

www.techweb.com/netbiz—internet business advice

www.anu.edu.au/people/Roger.Clarke—Roger Clark's huge Australian site on e-commerce

www.ecommerce1.com—general e-commerce site

www.internet.com/postmaster.htm—rental e-mail lists of willing recipients

Chapter S3
The Broadband Revolution

The years 1999 and 2000 saw the emergence of a new phenomena for internet communications—low-cost, high-speed access to the internet. The quote of the time was that "anyone still dialing up the internet is a dweeb." The need to connect to the internet from a dial-up modem was quickly passing.

Instead, three new methods have emerged offer the individual and small business full-time, high-speed access to the internet. They are cable modems, wireless networks, and Digital Subscriber Lines (DSL). The impact of these new services are so great that you, as IS manager, must pause and reconsider the wisdom of connecting your local area networks to the internet over dedicated digital lines.

For example, the cost of a T1 digital line is around $1,200 a month, yet you can obtain the same 1.5 megs a second for about $200 on wireless or DSL services. Better still, cable modems can top out at 10 megs a second for roughly the same price. So, why should you switch?

To determine the best connection option for yourself and your company, you need to understand the three new options. All three offer benefits and disadvantages. Knowing these will ease your decision making.

The Wireless World

A good place to start is with wireless internet access. This is the most unique of the options with the least amount of standardization. We should also introduce a concept called the "last mile." Telecommunications companies tend to carry the backbone signals of the internet. These are sent to major distribution center and internet service providers. The connection to your home or business is handled by other companies. This final connection to you is known as the "last mile." A new generation of companies, technologies, and ideas are fighting to control this last mile. It is too early to tell who, if anyone, will win the battle. On the other hand, the fight should create opportunities for you such as lower prices and better service.

With wireless access, an internet service provider, telecommunications company, or a communications start-up company installs a transmission tower in your area. You, in turn, purchase a receiving antenna and the receiver/transmitter needed to provide two-way communications. A microwave signal is beamed to your location where your receiver picks up the signal and sends it through a processing computer, router, and any other necessary equipment. The signal contains a stream of information from the internet requested by the transmitted signal from your office. In short, microwaves take over for phone line connections.

The first problem you have with wireless is that there are many different varieties of systems already in place. Wireless First in Traverse City, Michigan uses a 2.8 gigahertz signal with a range of 60 miles to provide internet access at speed from 256kbs to multiple T1 speeds. In New York City, WinStar uses 38 gigahertz frequencies to deliver T1 speed access to various customers. The signal is so high in frequency that the sending and receiving antenna's have to be pointed directly at each other.

Hybrids also exists. For example, DirecTV can provide you with 400kbs reception of internet information through the 18-inch satellite dish on your roof. However, you need to use a 33.6kbs or 56kbs modem hooked to a phone line to send out your requests for data. Therefore, your upload stream is much slower than the download stream.

However, wireless offers several advantages. The first is that all the information is being sent as digital packets. This allows the same signal carrying data to also carry voice communications. Specifically, telephone service for your company. For example, WinStar's system can transmit to a single site up to 250Mbs and 3,360 phone lines at the same time. Thus, your phone and internet system can be combined at one low price.

Another major advantage with wireless is that your internal networks can also be wireless. Each computer is given a transmitter/receiver card or device with an antenna. Internet information flows into your main receiver which uses a router to send the data to the appropriate computer via wireless signal. Then when a person moves his or her office to a different department, they just pick up the computer and move it. There is no need to move wires or re-route signals.

Wireless also gives you the ability to hook up laptops to receive the signal within the transmission area. Take the example of a law firm located in downtown Chicago. A lawyer starts his day at home in Skokie browsing internal memos and the internet. Stuck on the freeway, he continues to review case briefings received by the laptop. At the office there is no need to plug into the network because the wireless signal is automatically recognized. Several blocks down the street at the Federal Court House he is still in touch with the office's virtual network and the internet.

Wireless First and Northwestern Michigan College have a bus loaded with computers hooked to a wireless network and internet connection. It can roll into any business in Grand Traverse County and give internet training classes without the need to hook up to a phone line. It can also be located at a company to give them temporary access to very-high internet service for temporary applications such as teleconferencing. You need 384kbs of access (two-way) to carry on teleconferencing at 30 frames per second with excellent audio and data sharing capabilities.

On the other hand, there are some disadvantages with wireless. The biggest problem is that you have to stay within the wireless service area. The communications tend to be line-of-sight. Therefore, you need a clear path of reception. Communities in mountainous regions or with high-rises tend to have trouble with reception. Also, if a person travels out of range, they are out of luck.

Cable Modems

Cable modems rely on the existing infrastructure of cable television service. The same coax cable that brings television into your home or office can also carry packet signals from the internet. However, this requires the cable company to install complicated equipment to make internet access service possible.

Once installed, the cable company sets up local networks by neighborhood. Thus, many households or several businesses are linked as if on a local area network. To gain access you install a cable modem. You treat the cable modem like a regular modem. The difference is that this modem is always connected to the internet. Theoretically, you can receive up to 40Mbs. However, because you are connected in a group, the actual rate will depend on the demands of the other group members. Therefore, you may find yourself with actual speeds at 1Mbs or less.

Worse yet, you will need a firewall for your cable modem. Because of the local area network node created by your local group, you now have people from outside your company having direct access to your systems. Without protection from intruders, you could find your neighbor looking through the files on your computer.

Cable modems do have the advantage of being inexpensive to buy and install. A wireless connection, in contrast, can require up to eight new computers being installed at your site to handle the routing of traffic. Also, the cable infrastructure is already in place in many locations. Wireless tends to concentrate in urban areas.

Digital Subscriber Lines (DSL)

The real threat to both cable modems and wireless comes from DSL service (see Figure S3–1). This high-speed connection uses your existing phone lines to bring in internet access. Using the spectrum not used to reproduce the human voice, DSL can bring in up to 1.5Mbs over an existing single phone line. In addition, you can still use the same line to place phone calls while your computer is connected to the internet.

You have to live or work within three miles of a telephone switch facility to get DSL service. In addition, because there is no standard way to install it, many times you will find that several companies are involved with installation. This can lead to long-delays in installation, frequent outages, and service problems.

However, the popularity of DSL is growing faster than the other two options. The DSL industry is also working on turnkey solutions for installation. Customers like the service because no new wires are brought in, speeds of 384Kbs are available for less than $50 U.S. a month, and you can still send faxes or making phone calls on the same line. Therefore, the small business and home office worlds love DSL.

Figure S3-1. Growth of DSL and Cable Modem Subscribers

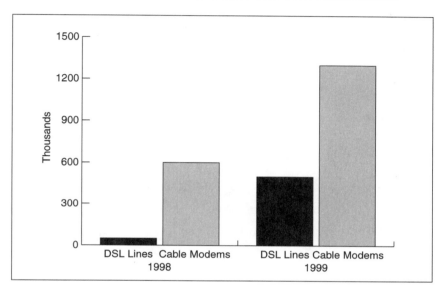

How Do The Highspeed Methods Work?

By understanding how these new broadband systems work, you will be able to make a better choice on what you want to do at your own company. Each system has strengths and weaknesses. All systems are still in development. When completed and perfected, they will be the next revolution on the internet.

Wireless

In the world of wireless internet connections there is no single standard. Whatever frequency and method of delivery that works is used (see Figure S3–2). In the United States, the broadcasters of digital information are usually confined to specific radio frequencies that were licensed by the Federal Communications Commission. These tend to be in the gigahertz range of the radio spectrum.

Figure S3–2. Wireless Internet Connections

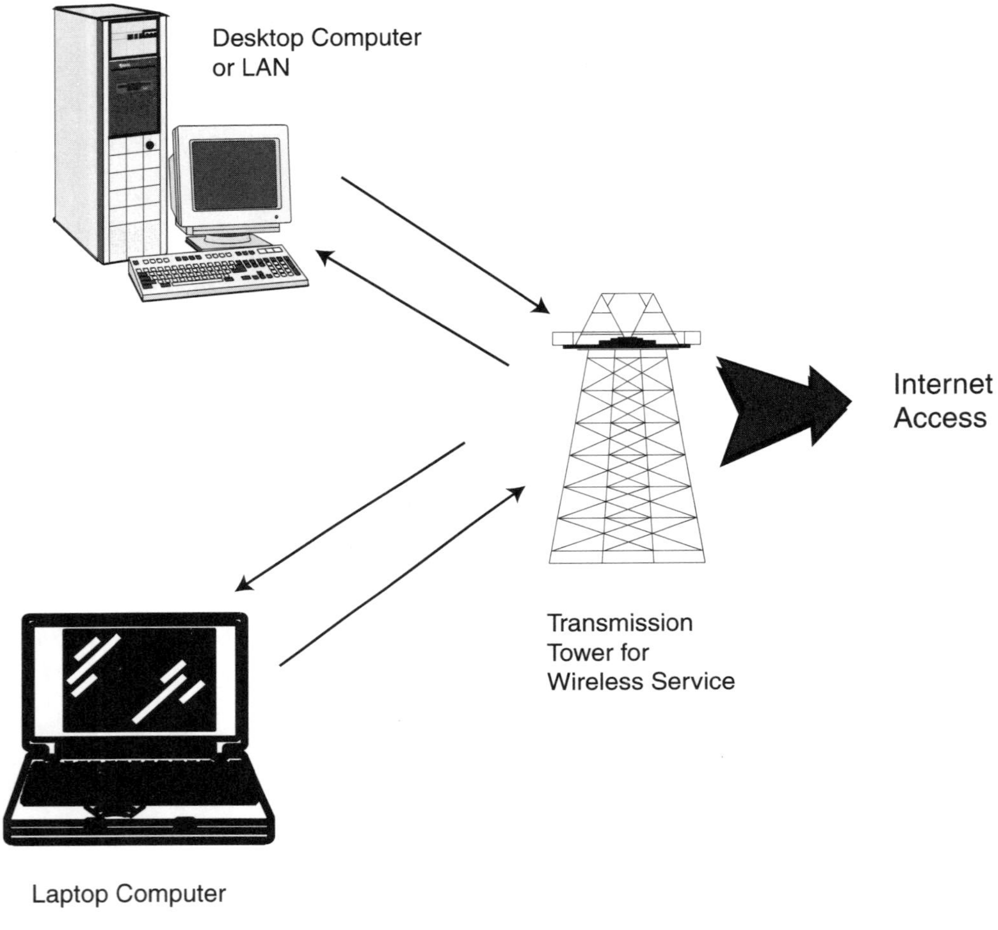

Desktop Computer
or LAN

Internet
Access

Transmission
Tower for
Wireless Service

Laptop Computer

This high of a frequency can only be used for line-of-sight communications. Therefore, each transmission tower must be visible to the receiving antennas. Trees, rain, and buildings tend to block or interfere with the signal. Therefore, cities surrounded by higher terrain tend to be good choices for this type of system. Traverse City and parts of San Francisco both have high hills nearby.

The sending of data from the user up to the network is referred to as "upstream." Data flowing from the network to the user is called "downstream." On any high-speed device, the first thing you look for is the upstream and downstream speeds being delivered. With a typical wireless system you get upstream and downstream speed choices. This can be combinations such as 64Kbs/256Kbs, 256Kbs/256Kbs, or 256Kbs/784Kbs.

What you need to do is evaluate the balance of upstream and downstream traffic in your company. If your users spend most of their time downloading files and images from the internet, a fast downstream speed with a slower upstream flow would make sense. If you teleconference, an equal upstream and downstream flow at a high rate would be your choice.

Wireless can offer both upstream and downstream speeds of 1.544Mbs. With additional hardware speeds, up to 20Mbs are possible. However, you need to have a site survey conducted to determine whether your location can receive the signal adequately. The antennas used are a few feet in length with wire loops or look like small microwave receivers.

The signal is sent in spread spectrum so that the actual frequency of the signal is changing two or three times a second. This makes eavesdropping harder, but not impossible. Therefore, you will want to consider adding other frequency changing options and encryption, where possible, to your feed.

Costs vary and are decreasing. For example, in California, it is easy to get 512Kbs downstream and upstream speeds for about $400 a month. This is much less that the price of a half-fractional T1 delivered by dedicated phone line. 256Kbs speeds can be had for under $200 a month.

Cable modems

A conventional modem modulates and demodulates signals over a phone line. This gives you top speeds of around 56Kbs. A cable modem is different. It is a true digital device that can work with the digital packets of the internet directly. Specifically, the cable modem is a radio frequent device capable of delivering up to 30 to 40 Mbs of data in one 6-MHz cable channel. The data is modulated using a QPSK/16 QAM transmitter with data rates from 320 Kbs up to 10 Mbs.

This allows the network headend to set transmission speeds to match the needs of the customer. A business should get a guaranteed rate at a high speed. Residential users can expect variable speeds with low upstream speeds. It is not uncommon that the local network will force upstream and downstream rates of data transmission to less than 100Kbs.

At the same time, you can be limited to using the cable modem for your own local area network. In the best circumstances, 16 users can be connected to a single cable modem. This is assuming that your provider is willing to let you hang a router to the cable modem. And, don't forget to include firewall protection because your network would be visible and accessible by others on the cable's network (see Figure S3–3).

Yes, you can still get television from your cable while using your cable modem. A simple splitter can hook up both the cable modem and a television. This is a point to remember when setting up home offices for employees and at the corporate office. If someone slips a TV card into their computer they get full cable television access on their monitor. This should be discouraged on the grounds of productivity.

At the cable company, they are using devices such as a cable modem termination system (CMTS) to control the flow of incoming data and returning data. An element management system (EMS) controls the configuration of the CMTS. This allows the cable operator to set up the number of users in a node and other parameters.

You should be aware that a large legal battle has been going on with cable providers and internet service providers. The ISPs want to be able to lease the cable lines to deliver their services. So far the cable people have not allowed this. Currently, the phone companies let ISPs use their infrastructure to deliver internet access. The outcome of this dispute will determine the number of choices and cost you will pay for cable internet access.

Also be aware that many cable modem systems are operating like an Ethernet WAN. Thus, the cable companies have the same abilities as a corporate WAN operator of a ethernet. This includes adding more data channels, nodes, and users. In addition, the data signals are encrypted and three different security layers are in place. This allows the cable company to make sure that only you get the data intended for you. It also reduces the chance of another cable data subscriber monitoring your data stream. It also reduces the chance of someone pulling cable television signals they didn't pay for.

One possible future improvement would be a switch to asynchronous transfer mode (ATM) over the cable system. This would give you the ability to send and receive television, data, and telephone through the cable. However, this would require a very expensive upgrade of the cable company equipment. Only major cities can expect this type of service.

Figure S3-3. Protecting a Cable Modem Connection

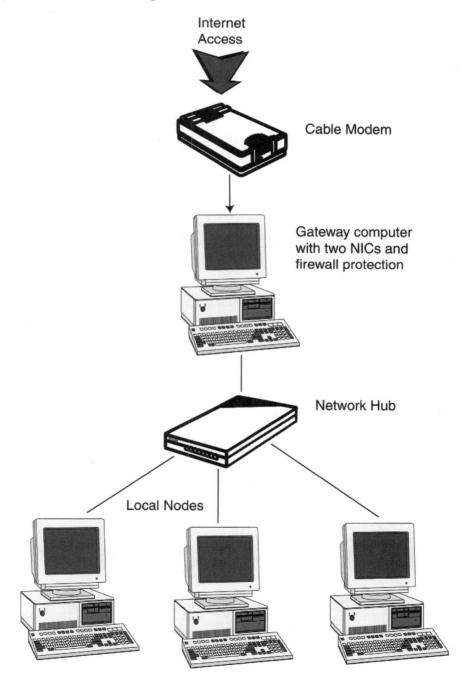

Internet
Access

Cable Modem

Gateway computer
with two NICs and
firewall protection

Network Hub

Local Nodes

The good news with cable modems is that standardization is better developed than with wireless. A coalition of communication companies have formed a set of standards and certifications known as the DOCSIS. This is currently controlled by a group known as the CableLabs. You can get up to date information on these standards and their certifications at the Cable-Labs site:

www.cablemodem.com

This system allows cable companies to have some degree of interoperability. This will eventually make cable modem service more predictable and easier to understand.

DSL

Digital Subscriber Lines come in a lot of flavors and hold great promise for the near term. They cannot match the speed potential of wireless or cable modems, but they are the current preferred method for high-speed connections. The reason for DSL's popularity is simple—it uses the same copper phone lines already strung into your home and office. Installation is just a matter of hooking up a modem device to the phone line. The telephone service is still available while you are using the line for data transmissions and reception.

However, DSL also have many limitations. To understand these we must look at the way that DSL works. First, there are different names for DSL service. Each represents either different standards, methods, or equipment used. Here are some examples,

1. *ASDL—Asymmetric Digital Subscriber Line.* One of the most common forms of DSL. It is a duplex system that sends and receives data at the same time. The downstream path is typically much larger than the upstream path. Downstream maximum speed is around 6.1Mbs, while upstream maximum rate is 640Kbs.

2. *CDSL—Consumer DSL (a Rockwell copyrighted system of DSL service).* It is cheaper and easier for phone companies to deploy but has lower upstream and downstream speeds than ADSL.

3. *DSL Lite—a simpler version of ASDL.* It does the data splitting at the telephone company site. Thus, it is inexpensive to deploy and install. It can reach from 1.544Mbs to 6Mbs downstream speeds. Upstream speeds can reach 128 to 384Kbs.

4. *HDSL—High bit-rate DSL.* This system is designed for distribution of high-speed data within a corporate site or between telecommunications sites. It has equal downstream and upstream speeds on a balanced line. Therefore, you can get up to T1 speed (1.544Mbs) in both directions.

5. *RADSL—Rate-Adaptive DSL.* A system that monitors line conditions and adjusts the rate of data exchange accordingly.

6. *VDSL—Very high data rate DSL.* A developing standard that allows speeds of up to 55Mbs over distances of up to 1000 feet. A technology to keep your eye on.

Except for VDSL, you have to be within 12,000 or 18,000 feet of the telephone company switching station equipped to deliver DSL. This is what limits the availability of the service. Also, the number of cities with DSL service is growing, but not all areas are covered. Small towns and industrial locations in rural regions cannot expect the service anytime soon. You can reach a DSL service by extending the communication loop with fiber-optic lines.

DSL works in a unique and simple way. Your ordinary phone line uses analog technology to convert your voice into signal and pitch. This is sent in analog form to the receiving phone. A modem converts data from digital form to an analog signal to be sent over the phone line. This limits speeds to as high as ISDN service's 128Kbs.

Thus, your phone line uses very little of its capability to transmit and receive the analog voice signals. DSL takes advantage of the unused capacity. Keeping the signal digital and sending it down the line increases the maximum theoretical rate to tens of megabits per second.

However, at some point the analog and digital signals have to be split to go down the same phone line. ASDL service puts that splitter at the home or office location. This adds expense and installation complexity. Other forms of DSL can put the splitter at the phone company office.

This is all well and fine, but today there is no turnkey solution to making the connection. Instead, someone has to install equipment at the home or office. Someone else has to set the digital signal rates. Still another person has to activate the switching system at the telephone company. The result is that several people have to coordinate their efforts for a quick and successful DSL installation. Many customers complain of having to wait days for the system to be up and running.

To provide you with DSL service, the local telephone company uses a Digital Subscriber Line Access Multiplexer. The DSLAM connects to an asynchronous transfer mode system to allow the phone company to have backbone connections to the internet at gigabyte speeds. Therefore, administration tends to be less expensive and capable of reaching large areas of customers. This results in current DSL service with internet access to start at about $49 a month.

Which to Choose?

The critical point with all three options is the ability to use routers and assign IP addresses. A dedicated digital line allows you to freely distribute IP addresses in your existing local area networks. You can direct all outgoing requests to the internet to one or more computers that handle the task. Incoming signals can be routed to the correct computer via its IP address.

Wireless service providers charge for more than a handful of IP addresses being used. Each computer that wants internet access needs a transmitter/receiver to either reach the internet, or the computer handling internet access. Cable modems limit IP addresses and sometime do not allow the connection of a router. DSL can only be split up to be shared by a few computers. Thus, the design of your existing system, the cost of changing to the new service, and the number of people needing internet access at high-speed determines which service you choose.

Therefore, your first step should be to survey your company to determine who actually needs high-speed service. We are assuming you already know the average access speeds users obtain using your existing internet connection. You will also need to know what times of the day the access will be used and for what applications.

Take the example of the marketing department and the production manager both wanting to use high-speed internet access to conduct teleconference with people all over the world. Both say that they will teleconference at least twice a week for up to four hours each time. By using the internet, the teleconference is essentially free and saves the cost of lost hours and expense because of travel.

If both groups use a single fractional T1 for teleconferencing, problems will result. Each will eat up 384Kbs of bandwidth. This will leave little or nothing for other people trying to access the internet. Plus, if a third party on the network decides to download a large file, it could interfere with the teleconferences. Therefore, one option is to install a single 384Kbs DSL line into a conference room and let each department schedule its use. As demand grows, more conference rooms can be provided with 384Kbs access from new lines.

Naturally, costs also have to be considered. Besides the cost of the high-speed connection, you will have to pay for internet access, equipment rental, and ongoing support.

Another consideration is the existing structure of your networks. Creative use of new data lines and redundant connections can enhance your existing access at a low cost. For example, the idea of redundancy can be applied. If your existing network is using a dedicated fractional T1 for internet access, you could change to two or three DSL lines from different carriers. Failure on one line would not impede service from the other lines. Access could be provided on the departmental level, instead of a corporate level.

Also, there is the issue of people within the business that will be working from home. Cable modems, wireless, or DSL can be available for most locations. However, you do not need as high of speed as the office lines. Therefore, you can compare costs, reliability, and other factors against an option like ISDN.

ISDN is available to us locally for $42.50 a month. This gives 128Kbs of service both upstream and downstream. For most home-based workers a 56Kbs modem is adequate for e-mail and small file transfers. For large file transfers and interactive applications, higher speeds will be needed. If teleconferencing or the sending of gigabyte sized files occur, 512Kbs and faster options will be needed.

A good example of this situation is the home-based video-editor or a video-editor located at a vendor's facility. Ten minutes of digitally captured video can create a file of 50 or more megabytes. Thirty minutes of video and sound can create gigabyte sized files. If you can transfer these fairly quickly back and forth for approvals, suggestions, and rendering, dozens of hours can be saved.

How to Actually Get the Service to Your Company

Even though these three forms of broadband communications exists, it doesn't mean they are available. Take our office as an example. We are located in a suburb of Grand Rapids, Michigan. About 100 feet in front of our offices is a fiber-optic cable carrying digital information. When we wanted a T1 line, the phone company only needed to tap into a junction box about 150 feet up the street and bring a copper cable into our office.

The process was messy and time consuming, but T1 service was available within three weeks of our placing an order. That was about four years ago. Now let's look at what happened when we looked into these alternative services.

First came the search for a DSL service. A call to every telecom company in our area revealed that only the downtown Grand Rapids area was expected to have DSL service available this year. The local phone station (about 1000 feet from our office) does not have the equipment for DSL. None is expected to be installed this year. A total of eight man hours were spent to find out that we couldn't get DSL.

Next, we went to the internet to check on cable modems. TCI provides cable service to our area. The internet site for TCI revealed that cable modems are not planned until the later half of this year. A call to the local TCI office confirmed this information. The good news is that when they come the homes of our staff members will also be able to get the same service. This will give us the ability to have a 1Mbs virtual network for our office. We can close down our wide area network that is using 56kbs modems.

The wireless people also revealed that the service is not available yet in our area. However, they are studying the possibility. A local loop would be installed at the local Quest office. To this they would hook the wireless tower for the whole city. This is located six miles from our office and is line-of-sight. Thus, if wireless is brought to the city, we can get our T1 speeds through the airwaves.

This same series of calls and internet checks should be performed by your office to determine if you have multiple choices and when service will be available. You will also need to know the costs involved. Our checksheets from the main volume will help you calculate your needed bandwidth and to plan for the bandwidth you want for the future.

Once you do find the service you want you can be pretty sure that installation and implementation will not go smoothly. The best example of this is with DSL service. The telephone company has to be notified and have its switching set up correctly for your DSL circuit. The internet provider has to link you to the internet. Phone wires and modems have to be installed and checked. If a mistake is made anywhere, the system doesn't work. Because several companies tend to get involved, about 40% of DSL users report initial problems.

Therefore you need to assign someone from your staff to monitor the entire process. If possible, have this person learn the installation procedures and what is being switched, activated, or connected. This will make the addition of more lines from the service go that much smoother the next time.

Next, be aware that advertised speeds don't mean you will get these speeds. Again, DSL is a good example. Connection speed depends on factors such as the distance you are from the local phone office, the quality of the line, electrical interference, and how well the modem you have synchronizes with the providers equipment. For example, a service advertised to provide 1.5Mbs of access might give over 7Mbs in one location and less than 1Mbs in another.

The best step is to negotiate a contract with the provider to test the actual equipment and lines before finalizing the contract. You may find that you get the 1.5Mbs speed, but packet loss rate and disconnection rates are too high for your standard of reliability. You should also test your system by sending a ping command and measure the lag time for a reply in milliseconds. You want less than 300 milliseconds for acceptable results and under 100 milliseconds for mission critical applications. Otherwise applications like videoconferencing can suffer noticeable lags in performance.

Another concern is the use of modems at your site. Many of the broadband modems come equipped with password protection so that you can log in remotely to check the system and set options. Unfortunately, these same modems come with a standard factory default password. Your first installation step should be to change or disable this password. Otherwise, it is a simple matter to gain access to your service by an outsider.

When you hook up DSL, you will need to select an internet service provider (ISP). Many of the telephone companies that install the DSL service also have their own ISP. This eliminates another party from the installation process. However, you still need to check the quality of the ISP for service, reliability, and technical support offered. In many cases you will already have an ISP for your company. This will require you to contact the current ISP to discover if they support the service you are about to install. If so, you will have to debate the merits and costs of the current ISP versus the telephone company ISP to make a decision.

The next issue is your IP address. With DSL and wireless you get a fixed IP address. Or, you can choose to have several fixed IP addresses. This gives you the flexibility to have your own web hosting or to set up several network users to the service. With cable modems that becomes a bit more problematic. Typically, the cable companies issue dynamic IP addresses so that you can't run your own web server from the connection.

Another effect you might experience is that some internet services don't work with your connection. For example, your e-mail program may run using port 25 for SMTP. However, your cable modem or DSL modem may have this port turned off. Or, it is possible that port 25 service is not available from your provider without a formal request. In either case, you will have to get the port turned on to get full e-mail service.

It is problems like these that make the installation of broadband internet connections annoying. However, the providers of DSL service are working hard to develop software and hardware solutions that will turn the process of connecting the service into a one-step task. Until then, the pain of installing the service is well worth the increased capabilities it represents.

Connections to Your LAN

Once you have a broadband service hooked up, tested, and implemented, it is time to think about how to connect it to the local area network. The best option is to connect the service to a select few computers for best results. Typically, this would be the people that need the constant internet connection at high speed to boost the productivity of their jobs.

Or, you may survey the company and find that you want to spread the high speed option to many or all staff members. In this situation you have to deal with the reality of the connection being shared by enough people to degrade its performance. For example, wireless can bring 1.5Mbs speed internet to your office, but if 30 people are using the service it tends to water down performance to 56kbs modem performance.

To connect the broadband cable or DSL line to your system you'll need firewall protection and a computer with a ISA 16 Bit Ethernet card with a RJ45 Ethernet port. Again, more problems may occur here. First, many cable and DSL providers won't allow you to hook the line into a Linux, Windows NT, or other operating system intended for server operations. The fear is that you will use the computer as a web hosting site or other ISP function.

Therefore, use a Windows Workstation or Unix Workstation computer to make the connection. The computer can have two ethernet cards and act like a gateway computer. Then you can send the incoming signals to several nodes on the net.

A Brief Word about Satellites

The big promise with broadband communications comes from satellites. With satellites you don't have to worry about service being available. Instead, you can have the service in any location. All you need is a dish antenna that can point up to the telecommunications satellite. Today, this is not the answer for broadband communications. Within five years all of that could change.

Today, you have only a few choices for this type of broadband communications. None of them are particularly well suited for a business application. For example, DirecPC is an excellent example of currently available services good for a limited business application. You install a 21-inch dish antenna on the roof of your building and a satellite modem either external to your computer using the USB port, or internally with a PCI card.

The upstream requests for internet content requests goes out over a convention 33.6kbs or 56kbs phone modem. The HTTP command is tunneled to the DirecPC node which calls up your requested content, beams it up to their satellite, and back down to the antenna on your roof. This gives you a downstream rate of up to 400kbs. However, the ping times extend to 500 or more milliseconds. In other words, the delay between request and start of content reaching your machine is up to one-half a second.

Any Pentium machine with PCI slots, USB ports, or both can be used for internet access. The 400kbs speed is fast enough to view streaming video at 30 frames a second and to receive large files much faster. However, you have to pay for the antenna and equipment (under $300 U.S.) and usage fees on top of your normal ISP costs. There is no way to increase the upstream speed, so you lose the ability to send large files quickly, teleconference, and several of the other benefits of broadband communications. Cable modems, DSL, ISDN lines, and wireless are about the same monthly price or less with much better bandwidths in both directions.

Satellite antennas can suffer loss of signal from intense rain or snow forming on the surface of the dish. With our satellite system we spend at least three or four days each winter throwing snow balls at the dish trying to free up an ice or snow buildup. For people in tropical regions the snow is not a problem, but the moisture content in most thunderstorms will block the signal. In addition, most satellite systems like DirecPC only support the Windows platform.

Now compare the current situation with one of the most famous and upcoming satellite systems planned for operation in 2003—Teledesic. This is a fleet of over 288 low Earth-orbiting satellites that will be launched around 2002 and onward. Teledesic is being built by Motorola and is supported financially by people like Craig McCaw and Bill Gates.

Once the system is in place you will be able to link both upstream and downstream with the satellite fleet from any point on Earth. The access speed is planned to be 64Mbps downstream and 2Mbps upstream. The cost is anticipated to be the same as today's broadband options. Millions of channels will be handled at the same time by the fleet. The frequencies and licenses for this project are already in place.

This type of a future means that broadband will soon be the standard for all internet connections within business. You will be able to have people carry their laptops anywhere in the world and still be hooked to your networks. ISPs will not be necessary. All the benefits of broadband will be available. This means that your company will have to keep this possibility in its five-year plans.

Applications That Become Possible with Broadband

When broadband is widely available, or if many of your current customers and users have broadband, just which benefits become available? And, what impact will that have on your planning and operation of your current networks?

First and foremost, existing web sites have to be redesigned to accommodate broadband applications. In the past we had to design web sites with an option for text-only for people with outdated browsers. Then we created multiple language sites to accommodate a world audience. Now we will have to design web sites with a "broadband option" to allow people with 256kbs and faster speed access to use the broadband applications.

One example of the power of broadband is that software applications can be stored on a web site and run with browsers. This is possible now, but with better throughput of data the result will be the ability to run software and store data on the internet, instead of each computer's hard drive. With the "always on" characteristic of broadband connections, this means you could feed live data to your customers day and night. This has the potential of turning the internet into the world's largest free market for products and services. Let's look at just a handful of the more interesting options that broadband will make possible.

Telephony

As we write this there is a race to introduce the first widely deployed voice-over-IP phone systems. Voice-over-IP means that the packet characteristics of the internet are being used to create digital phone systems that use the same IP protocol the internet uses. That means you can place digital phone calls down the same data line feeding your personal computer. Needless to say, this is serious competition for phone companies.

The promise of this technology is that you would be able to place long-distance calls using your computer. You could also integrate your PBX phone system in the office to use the internet for frequent point-to-point calls, such as between two branch offices. The cost of phone service would then drop.

Not so obvious is that you could include a phone option in your web site. A person scanning your catalog could punch a web page button and be talking directly to a technical person or sales representative. This creates a host of possibilities for any company. For example, you could set up teleconference sales demonstrations for potential clients. This would reduce the travel expense and time of the sales agents and engineers.

Also possible will be the connection of potential customers by phone over the internet to the closest dealership. In our own studies, we have found that about a third of current internet customers use the web to research a product and then call the store to place the order instead of using the online ordering form. They tend to feel more comfortable with the idea of dealing with a human directly. Therefore, you can now have two methods of instant ordering, one on the web site and one using voice-over-IP.

However, as the IS manager, you can quickly see that once again your job description has been expanded. Now you have to maintain a voice-over-IP phone system for your company. In addition, there is the matter of having people available to answer the calls coming from customers, suppliers, and joint venture partners. This new technology creates a second phone system in your office. Someone has to answer each call and route it appropriately.

Interactive marketing

Staying with our e-commerce theme, a broadband connection means that you can have interactive marketing. That is, instead of presenting your product or service on a web page with little feedback possible, you can now add video and audio without fear of chewing up your bandwidth.

Take the case of a company selling a product with many types of applications. A customer could select the application they have in mind and then be treated to a multimedia presentation of the product in use for their desired application. If one characteristic of the product catches their interest, a simple click of the mouse brings up more information.

We recently did this for an electronic goods retailer. Many customers were calling asking how particular digital cameras functioned. The store was spending three-quarters of their phone time on these questions. What they did was create two tracks of in-depth information. For low bandwidth users, one track showed pictures of the controls on the camera and explained what each one did. The second track was a video of a person using the camera while explaining how each control was set for each photographic situation. The second track was intended for the broad bandwidth capable customers.

It would also be possible to have a sales representative available eight hours or more a day to answer "live" questions from people browsing the site. Using streaming live video the representative could show each camera and go through the advantages of each based on audio or e-mail questions coming from the web site browsers.

In addition, regular demonstrations could be scheduled so that many potential customers could watch a product in action. This is the internet equivalent of the in-store demonstration. The difference being that you can reach more people anywhere in the world.

Streaming video

Let's take a moment and discuss streaming video for a minute. To present a video and audio presentation to many users on the internet you need to dedicate web servers to the task. There are even special web servers designed to present streaming video to multiple people at the same time. Typically, one of these servers can handle 60 users linked to the same video stream.

For corporate sites or popular web sites, this can mean the need for several streaming servers. In such a situation you need to cluster the servers so that if one fails, the next one in the cluster takes over. The size of the cluster will be determined by the number of people expected to call on a video source and how close to zero failed connections you wish to have. This also means you need to rerun your internet connection bandwidth calculations again to determine the total bandwidth needed to support your expected peak periods.

An application for streaming video, such as training videos for your staff located around the world, will put high demands on your internet system. Video tapes will need to be transferred into digital form and then compressed for internet transfer at 15 to 30 frames per second. Programs like Quicktime and RealAudio can accomplish the compression of a digital source. There are both programs, video capture cards, and dedicated PCs available for transferring and editing analog video and audio to digital formats.

Therefore, when someone proposes to put something like training videos on your internet site, be sure to budget for the time, people, software, and hardware to support this idea. Also make sure that upper management is aware of the commitment necessary to run such sites successfully.

Interactive TV

Digital video cameras have launched a revolution. For movie audiences it means that many feature films are now being shot in a digital format. Television stations can shoot broadcast quality footage with cameras as small as a handheld camcorder that costs under $4,000. As IS manager, it means that you can create your own television station on the internet.

Digital video cameras like the Canon XL1 can almost match Beta SP television cameras for quality. The XL1 is small and light, costing well under $4,000. The camera can record 30 frames per second of digital video or still images. These can then be downloaded through a firewire port (IEEE 1394) to a computer such as the Apple G4. The G4 has two firewire ports and built-in digital video editing capabilities. Thus, for about $5,000 a package you can have everything you need to create videos or a live video stream.

However, do not be fooled by the low price of the equipment. To make truly professional television shows you will need at least two cameras, tripods, dollies, lighting, studio, and most expensive of all, a good set of microphones. High-quality microphones start at several hundred dollars.

Still, with a budget of under $20,000 you can piece together a television studio. That way corporate announcements, press conferences, training sessions, product demonstrations, and the like can be transmitted live or recorded onto the internet. This opens up the possibilities that come with owning your own television station that can transmit around the world.

However, it also takes a staff to manage and produce programming. For example, someone has to edit together the video images with graphics, sound effects, titles, and other elements. Such a person typically earns $40 an hour and up in the real world and can be hard to locate.

A web site offering regular television broadcasting to customers can resell the content to the broadband content providers like Broadcast.com. Now your legal team is involved with contracts and negotiations. The lesson here is that for each powerful internet technology that comes from broadband capabilities, a new set of management issues arise. This requires you to go back to our book and recalculate your needs for resources. You also have to fight the allure of flashy hardware and software to first plan and implement the process correctly.

TV and internet on your television

The capability of creating television content brings up another aspect of this technology. Specifically, digital television opening the door to internet and broadcast signals both being received with one unit. In other words, you can soon watch television that allows you to click on the advertiser's web site address and open it in a separate window on the screen.

This allows your company to plant a 15, 30, or 60-second advertisement on television and have ready a web site to take thousands of people clicking through for more information. A good case study in this potential occurred when Victoria's Secret offered a sneak peak video of their newest products on an internet video. The television ad generated millions of hits to the web site. The video was slow and jerky, but widely watched.

With broadband and enough servers, this could have been a direct extension of the television advertisement. Many minutes of additional information could have been viewed by television watchers after the TV commercial was through. Thus, you get impulsive buyers going right to your site where shopping and ordering is possible. Or, you can counter bad publicity by having your side of a story run on a web site as soon as the news breaks.

Needless to say, this means that as IS manager you have to have web sites set up to take a sudden and massive inflow of interest. Hit counts can go from a few thousand to a few million in a matter of minutes. Having backup servers at an ISP to take up the pulse of requests is one way around the problem without having to invest in extra hardware.

File sharing

Broadband also means that very big files can be shared. As we pointed out earlier, this will enable people working on memory intensive applications (video editing, CAD, etc.) to do the work at home and quickly send it to other people in the corporation.

Now think about this scenario. You look away a moment at the airport and then discover your laptop computer is gone. On it is the entire presentation for your newest product. This is valuable information for a competitor. If you listened to our advice in the original book you would have encrypted your data and the plans would be safe.

Now envision that you still don't have the presentation. Thanks to broadband you can connect to a cable modem at your hotel and quickly retrieve megabytes of data using a rented laptop. The presentation is again in your hands.

Data backup

There is also the possibility of network-wide backup of data from any location on earth. On top of the regular backup of LAN servers and web servers to tape, you could also use your inexpensive broadband connection to send backup data to a data storage site on the internet.

One such system we designed had a cluster of servers delivering high speed content to the internet. A backup server was located across town at a different ISP. The cable modem in the office was used to send hourly backups of the web site's database to the backup server. Should a disaster such as a fire strike the first ISP site, we could redirect traffic to the second site and buy time to reconstruct the original cluster.

Staff members with laptop computers or working at home could have automatic data backups sent to your LAN server each time they log into the internet. In this way, you would be backing up their work as if they were still in the office connected to the LAN.

Likewise, broadband communications make it possible to have robust virtual networks on the internet. With 1Mbs speeds, you can have very flexible and mobile network users all sharing the same data sets.

Planning and Management of the New Possibilities

As mentioned earlier, the web site has to be redesigned. Adding broadband capabilities means changing the web site into two parallel tracks. One track sticks to our original rules about keeping a site simple, avoiding Java scripts and the like. This keeps the speed of bringing up the site quick for 56kbs and less modem users.

For the broadband group you still keep the clean and simple look of the site and ease of navigation. Fancy logos, animation, and the like are still shunned if they do not reinforce your site's message. Instead, you enable streaming video, two-way interaction, live updates, and audio contents to deliver a wider and deeper message to the person visiting the site. A classic example of this is the 360-degree view of a home made possible with broadband, digital cameras, and "stitching" software. Now the potential buyer can literally walk around a home and look around the neighborhood from their internet browser.

Before you proceed, you need to survey your customers and employees to see who has or can even get broadband service. The switch to broadband-based sites comes as you see the number of customers or employees with broadband access increase to significant numbers. The point of significance will vary by situation.

We recently polled the readers of a custom e-mail newsletter on international trade. We found that the base of 1,800 readers consisted of approximately 10% with cable modems or DSL service. Although a numerically small number, it still surprised our client and lead to the creation of internet broadcasts of the same newsletter content via streaming video. The customers receiving the service were delighted.

The client's perspective on this was that the investment in cameras and equipment were less than $1,000 thanks to patient eBay purchases. The delivery of streaming video news on a vertical market topic was a first in their area. Press releases on this capability helped to grow the subscription list and force competitors to make hefty investments to keep up.

As mentioned before, you still have to run through the planning for equipment, personnel, and software to accomplish the missions prompted by entering broadband broadcasting. These should be done using the same formula and project management steps we outlined in the main volume.

Issues with Broadband

Broadband is obviously the next step for the internet and its related technologies. However, this next step will not be painless. We have already seen that previous advancements in the internet has forced IS managers to broaden their responsibilities to areas outside the IS field (i.e., quality assurance, sales, marketing, telephony, etc.). Following are just some of the issues you will have to deal with when entering the broadband arena.

Added resources are needed

The user has it easy with a few hundred dollars for a special modem, set up fees, and monthly fees. The manager of a web site has to now produce the greater content such bandwidth demands. With streaming audio and video you need additional servers, backups, personnel, experts, software, and so on. With larger databases connected to your web site with expanded capabilities, you need server clustering to assure continuous connections at high speed.

Security becomes a major issue

Many users of broadband technologies forget that it also opens up new avenues for intruders into your computers. Always "on" cable modems are actually in local area networks run by the cable companies. Without firewalls, outsiders can get into that LAN and then your computer and perhaps your LAN. Personnel working from home are sending massive files back and forth from the office. Each pass is another chance for eavesdropping. Wireless connections can be monitored by outsiders. DSL lines going into homes can be tapped or hacked. Therefore, you need to build a first line of defense at each external machine that watches for attacks or intrusions.

You can go too far, too fast for your customers

One danger is that you can put too much content into your site and baffle your customer. You always have to keep in mind the customer's perspective. It is nice to see how to install a piece of special plumbing via streaming video. It is another to find that you have to click through several screens just to purchase the part. The priority is always to serve the customer and to keep e-commerce simple and inviting.

You can be left behind

The greater danger is being left behind. You could wake up one morning to find that your largest competitor is now producing hours of content for the

CNN/fn web site on your industry. Their products get most of the attention and thousands are tuning in to learn more. Your web site, in comparison, now looks very weak. Everyone in your industry is tuning into this internet content to learn of developments in the products and related regulation. They stay to purchase the products.

Recommended web pages

www.speedconnect.com—wireless information
www.dslreports.com—up to date reports on DSL service and availability
www.cablemodeminfo.com—cablemodem information
www.aspergantis.com/adsl/performance.htm—provides free bandwidth measurement tools

Search terms

DSL

xDSL

Wireless Internet

Cablemodem

Chapter S4
Security Revisited

In the main volume, we took a long look at how to write security policies, enforce security rules, and set up secure systems. However, security is a dynamic issue. For every new defense, a new offense seems to form. The Melissa virus of 1999 ripped through e-mail systems at many corporations. People were not well-educated on the rule that you don't open executable files in e-mail that you didn't request. The denial of service attacks on the internet in early 2000 also illustrated an attack that quickly overwhelmed defenses. In this case, the affected sites were able to stop future attacks quickly. Credit was given to an existing reaction plan for such problems.

In another publicized account, someone broke into an e-commerce site and stole thousands of credit card numbers. The affected company did the prudent thing and canceled all of the cards. However, imagine the customer satisfaction in learning that your credit card was just canceled because of a mistake someone else made. Therefore, as IS manager, the job of preserving security increases a notch from when we wrote the original book.

The Layered Approach

In a perfect world you would have all day to work on security issues and stay up to date on threats. Unfortunately, you are already working 12-hour days fighting off dozens of different problems and attempting to keep your management team happy. Therefore, security tends to be addressed once in a corporation and then left alone for a very long time. This is the recipe for disaster.

Instead, you need to regularly review the security issues, even appoint a permanent security manager. You also need to address security at several different levels. There is the issue of the physical security of the network, the software security of the network, risks from outside users of the network, and thorough management of the system. Let's examine each of these separately.

Physical Security

As mentioned in the main volume, you always begin a discussion of security with a list of the potential threats to your system. To this we need to add a complete description of the system to be protected, especially where it begins and ends. At these points you will need to look at what level of protection is available outside of your system. The best way to crack a computer system is to get inside a company.

Therefore, you examine the overall security procedures at your company. If people are free to wander around the building without challenge or limit to access, a tight computer security system is required. If outside vendors can log into computers at the company that are connected to your network in any way, you have a major vulnerability to be addressed. If terminals connected to the internet are not logged off when not in use, you have another major issue.

Thus, you need to tie down the physical security of your system by making sure that all network related machinery is safe from fire, water, wind, dust, theft, and the like. The servers, routers, and switches of your system must be in locked areas with limited access. For example, the hub that controls the LAN in my office is out in the open. I plugged my laptop into the hub using a two foot CAT5 cable and quickly gained unchallenged access to my network. An outsider could have copied all accessible data files and walked away.

We will also repeat the golden rule of computers—always have a back-up. That means all data must be backed up and stored in a separate and safe location. For example, if you run a web server performing e-commerce, you should be running a mirror back-up to a separate server. The internet connection should be serviced by software that can instantly switch connections to the backup machine if the dedicated cable or your ISP suffers an outage.

In our situation, we co-locate our web servers at an ISP with extremely wide bandwidth. A dedicated and secured data line passes backup data to our office server. The ISP already has backup communication protection and daily data backup procedures. Our copy of the data comes in hourly and we are ready to re-route traffic to our machine in an emergency.

The Software Layer

The largest problem for security has been at the software level. Most of the internet-related security disasters have been the result of hackers taking advantage of weaknesses in the software. Take the example of a company that installs a Windows 2000 Server package and then hooks up a web site using IIS. The IS manager in this example is betting his job on the security of off-the-shelf products and nothing else.

What needs to be done is an installation of the latest software patches for the system. Therefore, you must constantly monitor your vendors for updated information on discovered security problems. The patches must be installed and updated as needed. Specific corrections to the system must always be taken. Most problems will result from neglecting a patch or upgrade.

Take the example of buffer overflow. In some programming languages you can enter information into a field that includes programming commands that the web site will dutifully execute. This flaw in several languages and protocols has been used to open access to systems or to overwhelm the site and bring it down. Worse still is that a well-educated attacker can gain access to hundreds of computer systems, install a trojan horse program, and have all of these systems attack a specific site. That would make your company an unwilling participant in an attack. If the victim is one of your vendors or customers the political fallout could be tremendous.

What is required at the software level is protection at the points of attack. Today that means the physical crossing points in your system, servers, routers, and switches. Any place where IP packets get sorted out, exchanged, or distributed is a key target for attacks. Therefore, each of these points must have its own form of protections. Let's review some of the possibilities for each point.

Point of connection

At one or more places in your system you have a connection to the internet. This is always the first place to install security measures. With dedicated data lines you can place a firewall system or computer with the router attached to the dedicated line. The router and the firewall systems can be set for the level of defense your site requires. (Remember, the type of site you run will determine your level of risk. Government sites, e-commerce sites, portals, or controversial companies are high on the attack list.)

A good firewall will perform two important functions. One is to filter out unwanted IP addresses and the other is to audit people probing your system. In some cases you can set a dynamic IP address for your router with a command to only let through validated packets from your ISP. This makes it hard for attackers to find and dwell on your router looking for a hole. A typical attack on a router is someone's script asking for permission from the various ports (e.g., port 25 for your incoming mail service).

The auditing program should be set to detect any multiple requests in a very short period of time. The probe of ports is a test to see if you left any "doors open." If such a probe is detected, your security software should sound an alarm and record the origin of the probe. Working with your ISP you have an outside chance of chasing down the culprit. However, it is very difficult to find most attackers, much less prove they are violating the law. Therefore, the strategy is to find the source of the attack and shut it off as far from your router as possible. If the ISP shuts off this account and IP address, the attack has to falsify a new account and still doesn't know which intended victim detected his presence. With enough discouragement an attacker will look for easier pickings.

Another good step at the firewall level is to translate IP addresses. All incoming IP packages are addressed to the firewall. Once approved a software routine re-addresses them to the correct computer within your system. Packets coming out of your system are retranslated to the firewall's IP address. All outsiders see is the firewall's address. They cannot "see" your internal IP addresses. If they could they would be able to piece together your addressing system and exploit your system.

Finally, you need to look for remote access capabilities on your routers and other equipment. Shut as many of these off as possible. A router with a capability to be reprogrammed remotely is a liability when not properly configured. Reprogramming of routers should only take place at the router or from a secure computer using a single, validated IP address. Again, you should set auditing software to monitor these features for tampering.

Switches

Switching hardware is a victim of attacks because they are usually left defenseless. When connecting together several LANs the switches are commonly left open to all traffic. Thus, an attacker can gain access to one LAN and gather log-ins and passwords for users on the connected LANs. Therefore, you want to limit traffic through the switches to authorized users only.

Servers

Once an attacker successfully enters a server, a world of potentially damaging information is available. Everything from passwords to credit card files can be obtained. Thus, the highest level of security is typically centered on the servers. This begins by limiting the capabilities of each server. For example, an e-mail server should have all non-related functions shut off. Unused ports that are left open are like unlocked doors to a building.

At the audit level, you should establish an alarm whenever anyone tries to access a port that has been turned off. At the same time you need packet filters in strategic positions within your system to ensure that traffic is coming from valid locations. For example, an internet-based packet is carrying the identification of an internal IP address is suspicious. The packet should be stopped and the audit trail started.

Encryption is strongly encouraged for sites serious on security. Encryption of messages, databases, and command codes are a minimum. Services like SSL only protect the messages passing back and forth on the internet. The collected data on your server can still be unencrypted. Or, try this experiment. Next time you need a password to log into a web site, look at the URL box and see if your password is being clearly displayed in the requested address. This is all an attacker needs to see to gain access.

Now, to pull all of this off you need to be consistent and diligent. Consistent in conducting at least monthly audits of the error logs and security logs of your servers and other systems. Look for things like unauthorized access attempts, normally sound programs returning odd error messages, multiple password attempts, and the like. This is evidence of an attacker working on your system.

Diligent means that you are thorough in setting up your security system. In larger systems this can be quite a headache. You need to know which groups need access to which services. Once the pattern for these is established you then must go through the entire setup again to look for weak points. This requires you to think like an attacker. You need to look for holes in your security system and plug as many as possible. Then you have to test the entire system to make sure that everyone granted permission for access is indeed getting the proper access. It never goes smoothly so you repeat this cycle a few times and only make compromises as infrequently as possible.

If you are really serious about security you live the hacker's life. Typically you appoint someone on staff to make weekly visits to the discussion sites for hackers. Learn how they think, what they like to target, and the tricks they learn. Use this knowledge to look at your own system. The weaknesses in systems will be discussed at these sites first, long before a security patch will be available for your system.

You will also want to stay tuned to the security sites that have daily updates on problems detected in the internet world. For example:

- *www.cert.org*—has a wonderful update service, newsletter, and white papers on security issues.
- *www.interhack.net*—discusses a variety of security topics.
- *comp.risks*—is a newsgroup dedicated to discussing security risks.

Search engine searches on keywords such as "internet security," "firewall," and "hackers" will lead you to other interesting sites. However, be very careful on downloading any software from these sites as they are typically under attack themselves by people trying to be more clever than the experts.

Strategies and Tactics

Let's take some specific concerns about security and discuss the strategies and tactics that would be used to counteract the threats. For example, let's start with a common threat—viruses arriving through e-mail.

The overall strategy would be to prevent any virus from getting into your system from the e-mail server. The key feature is that no virus gets into your e-mail service without detection. The greatest danger is that a virus would arrive into your system undetected. It would then have the capability of replicating itself into other parts of your internet system before the detection would occur from service failures or other symptoms.

On a tactical level, this strategy needs to be implemented by selecting specific locations, times, and situations that need to be addressed with specific countermeasures. Let's look at locations and see how our tactical approach is applied.

1. *The users.* The end users of your internet system are probably mixed in with the users of the local area network. Therefore, there is first and foremost a great need for training and awareness for the employees. They need to realize that they are one of the monitoring systems you depend upon to report possible virus attacks. For example, they must be trained to not open file attachments on their e-mails they did not request. This is a particularly tricky situation because e-mail can carry copies to other recipients bearing the name of someone from your company. Assuming that it came from an internal source, most people will open the infected file without thinking twice. Your job is to make these people think twice.

2. *The e-mail reader.* Each computer attached to the internet or an internet service will usually have a program for collecting and reading e-mail. Modern virus detection software can work with these programs to scan for infected files. For example, in McAfee VirusScan you can set up the V-Shield portion of the program to actively scan each e-mail attachment for viruses. However, this has to be done manually for each machine. At the same time, this does give you 100% protection, but it will provide many cases of early warning of a virus arriving at your company. From that point you need to have a reaction plan for how you will notify the users to watch out for the attack, as well as how you plan to search and clean the system.

3. *E-mail server.* E-mail will be received at a server within your company. This is where you should concentrate your anti-virus systems. This includes virus scanning software, audit trails, activity monitors, and other software solutions that could alert you to either an attack or a probe before an attack. At the same time, you need to carry out firewall protection of this server because it represents one of the gateways into your protected community.

4. *The ISP.* Your provider of internet services should also be working to prevent a virus attack. This will include scanning for viruses on their internal network and the scanning of the internet flow for problems. Someone at your company should also be on the alert for pending attacks. Monitoring of hacker sites and the daily computer press is encouraged. If your company is about to launch a controversial product or if a major political problem encourages attacks on your type of company, you need to have a plan for how you will beef up security.

5. *Management.* Finally, you, as IS manager, and other members of the management team must be an active part of the protection plan. Policies have to be in place to make sure that an internal employee does not feed a virus deliberately into your system. This would include publicizing the legal consequences of such an action and the strength of your system in tracking down such a malicious employee.

In addition to these types of standard procedures for addressing security needs for particular locations, you can also practice some unconventional methods. For example, deception technology can be deployed. Take the example of an employee detecting a virus from the outside. Although it is nearly impossible to track down the source, you release a brief e-mail hinting that the person was found and being prosecuted but not to mention this outside the company. The result is that internal employees believe that your system is even stronger than you indicated and are dissuaded from attempting a similar attack.

The Spam Threat

A major threat to security that is nearly impossible to stop is spam e-mail. Although most companies do not see it as a security threat, in reality it is a substantial threat. The damage is done in the time, bandwidth, disk space, and productivity lost to spam. Let's look at a specific example, a vacation get away offer that arrives by fax and e-mail to a few users in your company.

If the fax was printed out on paper, then fax time and paper were wasted. Worse still is the case where an employee makes dozens of copies and starts passing them around. More time and paper is wasted. If an e-mail arrives with the same offer and is 8Kbytes in size, each copy made wastes that much more disk space. For really busy e-mail systems, this can quickly add up to the mailboxes at a desktop computer getting so large it slows down the entire operating system.

Therefore, you need to look at similar locations as the virus threat to reduce spam as much as possible.

1. *The users.* Again, there is a need to educate the users on the threat spam e-mail poses to productivity. Stopping to read through a half a dozen worthless e-mails can burn five to 10 minutes of time each day. Multiply that

by the number of employees in the company and the days worked per year and you are wasting some serious time. Education will teach employees to skip over the obvious "junk" messages.

2. *The e-mail system.* Luckily there are now several software products available that allow you to screen out e-mail by keyword and sender. This will not stop all of the messages, but it will cut them down. For example, keywords such as "lottery," "hot girls," and the like can screen out some of the more obvious problems. However, these have to be used with care. Take our vacation offer above. If we screened out the word "vacation," employees e-mailing in vacation requests from home may find that the message never arrives. Therefore, the better approach is to mark the sources of spam e-mail by the origin address and screen them out. This prevents both current and future messages from that location.

3. *Management.* Believe it or not there is a law against unsolicited faxes (Title 47, Chapter 5, Subchapter II). As a standard management procedure, we have a copy of the portion on faxing highlighted stationed at every fax machine. A message on the bottom tells the sender to please remove us from their bulk fax list. This is sent in response to any junk fax. It is typically effective.

Naturally, you balance your attack on spam e-mail in proportion to the threat. This is not your highest priority, but it does deserve some time each month to cut down its volume.

New Sources of Attack and New Holes in Your System

At least a couple of times each year you should stand back and look at your complete security system. Security threats are dynamic and changing. The first problem is that people are constantly finding new ways to defeat security systems or cause problems for internet users. The second problem is that new services and features sometimes mean new openings into your computer system. Let's take a closer look at these two problems.

First, a new service like DSL or cable modems means that you have a new gateway into your network. Hooking an unprotected DSL line to a network-based computer means that outsiders now have an unprotected gateway into your system. This is a problem we have already addressed. Now think about the growing use of wireless connections to the internet. Literally hundreds of employees could be in the field using their Palm Pilots and pocket PC devices to download infected files. Once back in the office they cradle their devices to synchronize with their desktop computer. One unprotected machine and you have a virus loose in your system.

Again, education and the proper deployment of anti-virus software is a good start to preventing this problem. Employees should be made aware of the threat of downloading files from untrusted sources. At the same time, files being transferred into a computer from the USB or Serial ports should be scanned.

Now, think about an even larger problem—the employee's Palm Pilot is stolen at the airport. On the system is the log-in name and password for accessing your network's e-mail system. Now the thief has a valuable piece of information. The access can be sold to a competing company that can open and read confidential e-mail. Or the thief can do this and sell important information to competitors or release product information to the press.

Preventing this situation is even harder because the employee can go for one or more days before discovering the loss. In our office, all laptops and hand-held devices are not allowed to store passwords. It is up to the employee to enter the password for access each time the device is used or an outside connection is requested. Then a thief will have a very difficult time trying to crack through the security. This buys the time we need for the employee to report the loss and let us change or shut down accounts.

The other problem for your security system is that new ways are always being found to get around existing security systems. One way to handle this is to be a moving target. New security configurations and updates can be added to your system at regular intervals. That way the openings in your system keep moving around or they shut suddenly. This makes outside attack more difficult.

Being aware of problems at other companies is a very good defense. When the first "denial of service" attacks occurred in 2000, smart companies promptly called either the affected company or their computer consultants to learn how the attack was carried out and what prevented future attacks. One of the companies brought under attack actually had predicted the possibility of such an attack. The network monitoring software sounded an alert when an unnatural number of "ping" commands suddenly appeared. They shut down the "ping" service and cut off the attack before it could bring down their system.

Point of Connection

Finally, let's take a look at one location in particular, the point of contact with the internet. It cannot be emphasized too strongly that if your company decides to connect to the internet you need to make several determinations first:

- Why are we doing this?
- How will we connect?
- What do we hope to accomplish?
- What are the threats?
- How do we prevent security breeches?

Always start with the reason you want to connect. Specifically, what was it that prompted your company to want to hook to the internet. Perhaps the company wanted to be able to send e-mail to remote locations. Maybe you wanted to establish a strong internet presence. Then again, you could be setting up your Enterprise Resource Planning (ERP) using the internet, including electronic payment.

Each of these three example situations involve tremendously different levels of exposure and complexity. For each situation you must respond with an appropriate level of planning. A well-designed plan will account for your security needs and the strength of your system.

The next issue is how you will be connected. We have already talked about the issues surrounding the type of connections (i.e., DSL, T1, cable modem, etc.). What is to be addressed here is how that connection is made to your network. You can establish an independent network of computers to be used just for the internet. A strong firewall between this network and the internet is adequate in most situations. An intruder would not be able to get to your internal network. Management of the internet system would include the banning of use or storage of sensitive information on the internet dedicated computers.

However, most companies will need to have a link between machines dedicated for talking to the internet and part or all of your internal network.

In this case you will want to look into the usual firewall between the connections to the internet and the routers. At the same time you want a really strong gateway system between the internet computers and the rest of your internal network. Typically, a router would be used to send internet-related traffic to either your web servers or the internal network. A firewall would be put between that router and the internal network. Additional measures are also possible.

Next comes the question of how much you want to accomplish because you are hooked to the internet. The company that only wants e-mail service would manually shut off web, ftp, and other unrelated services. In addition, its presence on the internet would be nearly invisible. Thus, many security measures would not be needed. In contrast, a company with a strong presence on the internet needs to add a lot of security features to fend off attacks.

However, the security measures have to be designed so that the goals to be accomplished by the company are not restricted by the system. A company that wants a large sales force that can pick up price information from any location using the internet will not be able to easily restrict IP addresses that are allowed into the system.

Naturally, you also take the time to look at the number and level of threats that are presented to the system. This should be a critical part of your planning process. If necessary, you can rank each threat by the likelihood that it will happen times the potential damage it could cause. This will allow you to prioritize the threats that absolutely have to be addressed versus the trivial threats.

Finally, there is the question of how to prevent a security breach, as opposed to reacting once a breech is detected. This is a management-level activity. Preventive actions involves management reviewing the entire computer system. This is the process of collecting information about the system from many sources. This can include audit reports, incident reports, logbooks, interviews with operators, control charts, and the like.

From this, management must create a picture of what is possible in the way of security breeches within your system. As IS manager, you must supply a list of the various ways people can intrude on your system. For example, how do you know that the top managers' authorization keys for e-mail have not been copied? Working together you look at potential threats and plan actions to prevent the threats from becoming a reality. In the case of a major e-commerce site, this can be a full time job.

A Specific Example—Malicious HTML Tags

There are many examples of how security on the internet can be compromised. Let's look at one specific example to see how it works and how you would work to prevent it from affecting your system.

A little-known trick with web pages is that you can plant executable scripts within an HTML tag. A web page that allows a user to write out their own HTML message will also allow an intruder to plant a script in the message. The next user of the page will execute the script. This can pass viruses or other problems to users through web page links, e-mail, or newsgroup postings.

This type of a problem has to be attacked in several ways. First, you have to educate your personnel not to fill out HTML messages on other sites. This will involve educating them on the potential dangers. Second, you have to train people to be careful when exploring new newsgroups or untrusted web sites. Web sites of suspicious nature should be blocked by your access control.

At the same time, you must have your virus detection software set at each workstation to alert you of a problem. Quickly checking the log and history files of the web browser and other internet software in use should allow you to pin down the source of the attack. In this way you can quickly shut off access to the accused site.

Also, having reaction plans in place will help you to control the damage done by any form of successful intrusion into your system. Management must work to ensure the problem won't occur again. The damage down must be repaired and the work force educated to prevent a similar incident.

What Can an IS Manager Do?

This leads to the question we have been referring to throughout this chapter—how is an IS manager going to be able to keep up with a world of growing threats? The answer is to use his or her existing resources wisely by following a carefully laid out plan. The idea is to attack the problem at many different layers.

This means the development of an architecture of security. Too many companies put a firewall in place and call that the security system. This may be fine for a small office with half a dozen employees. However, any company of size or a company with valuable data products to protect needs defense in depth.

As we have stated earlier, the first level of defense is the physical security of your network. Make sure that servers, RAID arrays, data back-up, and the like are behind locked doors with a security alarm in place. The best way to get data is to steal the actual computer.

The second level of defense comes at the routers, your first point of contact with the internet. If possible, also get the ISP to defend their routers. Use packet filtering to keep out unwanted traffic. Turn off the services you don't use or want, such as ping, traceroute, and the like. You should deploy a system of setting up IP addresses on your internal network that are not allowed to be used for addressing messages to the outside internet. This will deny the intruder the use of internal addressing to move around in your system or to imitate one of your users.

Next come the firewalls and packet filters used to keep out unauthorized traffic. What most IS managers forget to do is set the systems up to prevent attacks from being launched from within your system out to the internet. This prevents a trojan horse program from using your site to attack other sites. As attacks grow in number, the makers of firewalls get more clever in ways to block them. It is important to regularly update your firewall strategy to ensure that new forms of attack are denied.

Then you should design and place a proxy server on your system. This is a server that acts as an intermediary between your network and the internet. It takes your network one step further away from the internet. Only the proxy's address is available to the public. These should be paired with intrusion-detection systems. That way you can be alerted in real time to suspicious behavior coming from the internet.

These are just some of the physical steps you can take. There also are the issues of education and trust. You need to educate the work force on your security procedures and how they are to be used in daily internet activities. This includes the prompt reporting of unusual activity at the desktop.

Trust is the process of establishing secured links between groups on the internet. If you regularly depend on an outside web site for information, you should look into establishing dedicated or trusted connections. This can be done in any one of several ways, including the use of encryption and permission codes. That way only authorized users from your site are able to communicate with the trusted site. The trusted site, in turn, is able to detect others trying to interfere with the connection.

There Is Hope

Despite the daunting task this seems to present, there is hope for the IS manager. Internet users are beginning to recognize the basic weakness of the "walled city" approach to security. A better model is to band together to present an area wide defensive system. Several organizations are working to make this a reality.

One is the National Institute of Standards and Technologies (NIST) in the United States. They are working on several committees to establish a wider range of security options and practices. For example, they are working on Role Based Access Control where software will be able to assign individuals access control based on the role they play in a project in real time. As responsibilities change, the security system changes to allow access to new information while closing off access to data related to completed tasks. The cost and complexity of security is greatly reduced with this model.

NIST also works on the IPsec Project, an effort to provide greater levels of authentication, integrity, and confidentiality at the IP layer of the internet. This includes an updating of the current Internet Protocol. The goal is to secure the infrastructure of the internet and thus deny attackers a free reign of travel through the system. One way to do this will be to provide a central security policy for the entire internet or specific sections of the internet.

You can obtain more information by visiting the NIST computer security home page at:

Csrc.nist.gov

Another good organization to join and monitor is the International Computer Security Association (ICSA). Their web site is:

ncsa.net

This site lists the newest forms of security attacks and how to prevent them. It also discusses security administration and other important topics. They also provide software and certification services.

Summary

Security is still the major concern for e-commerce sites. Through a proactive plan by management, a company can prevent many types of attacks from within and without. At the same time, your company must have security policies, a reaction plan for security problems, and a regular review of security threats. Only by being active and dynamic can you secure your IS manager's job by demonstrating your constant ability to prevent disaster.

Chapter S5
Keeping the Job You Have or Creating the Job You Want

There is one basic problem that underlies all internet activities for companies—the lack of skilled personnel. This leads to two main effects. The first is that skilled personnel that you have tend to wander away to better opportunities. This includes the IS manager. The other effect is that finding skilled people is extremely difficult. In this chapter, we are going to briefly review strategies for how to keep people with your department and what to do if you decide to leave.

Why People Leave

The most widely held, yet often mistaken belief, is that money lures away the skilled computer people. This is not usually the case. Others think that the computer people are overworked and they "burn out." This is a bit closer to the truth. What is more accurate is to remember that because of personnel shortages and growing demand for internet services, everyone in your department is overworked.

However, many people put in 12 to 14 hour days and seem to enjoy it very much. The issue is not the work load. Instead it is the level of worker satisfaction. Take the example of a web page designer that is single, working his first professional-level job, and getting a lot of attention for his good work. He will tend to enjoy the job and stay on. Contrast that with a married programmer with two very young children who is required to work on weekends and gets little or no credit for her work. This person may work fewer hours but be very unsatisfied with her job, and therefore will leave for a better position.

The key fact to remember here is that the average internet-related job holder is under the age of 35. This age group does not hold earnings in as high of regard as previous generations. In fact, a good income is almost assured in this field. Instead, it is the lifestyle they adopt that matters. The type of clothes they wear, the car they own, and where they live, are all based on the image they want to generate instead of on simple economics. This could be seen in the early part of 2000 when gasoline prices in the United States almost doubled, yet the sale of large vehicles to consumers continued to rise.

Therefore, you need to spend time with each staff member and find what it is they are seeking from their job. It may be to use the latest technology, to create the hottest site on the web, or to have an office with cable television. Whatever it is you feed that reward to match performance. For example, we once needed to create a huge database for the internet. The local programming shop was back-logged for a year. When we mentioned that the result would be one of the largest retail sites on the internet, we had six volunteers, including the president of the company.

Why You Want to Leave Your Company

We cannot discuss this topic without mentioning the very real possibility of the IS manager leaving the company. Motivations for this also vary widely. Typically it is the long working hours, the lack of recognition by management, the constant frustration of trying to find adequate resources, or much more likely, the realization that IS manager is about as high as you can go at your company.

I talk every week with IS managers and listen to their frustrations and concerns. Typically, every manager I talk to will allude to the dream of starting their own software or internet company. They watch the news every day and see internet start-ups obtaining millions of dollars in capital. Their non-technical journals are filled with the stories of small internet companies being bought out and their owners becoming extremely rich.

One of my job functions is to take such start-ups through the venture capital process. I can verify that there is an abundance of money flowing into internet technology. A couple of venture capital funds have recently been set up to raise one billion or more dollars to invest in start-ups. These funds had to turn investors away. In another case, I have been turned away from investment funds because my client "wasn't asking for enough money."

Therefore, in this chapter, we are going to investigate a strategy you can use to either keep important people in your company or to satisfy your yearning to have your own business. The strategy is called a "spin-off." The name comes from the fact that your daily work can lead to discoveries that can be spun-off of your company to create a new business or a new line of products for your company. The most famous recent example of this is 3Com, whose Palm Pilot became so popular it was much more profitable to detach that department into its own company.

Typically, your operations will not create anything to that scale. However, you will find weaknesses or neglected areas on the internet as part of your work. For example, you could be the IS manager for a law firm and discover a new market in backing up databases from the courts. You might be the manager of an IS department for a major corporation and discover that your e-commerce approach is so unique and effective that you can patent the "look and feel" and license it to other companies.

Or, as mentioned, you may discover something for the internet totally unrelated to your job. You then face three choices. The first is to do nothing and go back to work. The second is to approach your company's management team and propose that you develop the new idea into a product or service line for your company. The third is to leave the company and develop your idea into a new company.

What follows is a discussion of the last two options. As you will see, much can go into making a new company. If done well, success is likely. Fail to be absolutely sure of any one step and you risk failure and the need to go back into a regular job.

Moving from Idea to Plan

A popular phrase these days is "do the math." In the case of starting your own company, the phrase is very appropriate. The first step is to sit down with a spreadsheet program and realistically figure out if the idea is viable. For example, you have an idea for a software program that will double your internet connection speeds without adding equipment. You want to give it away as shareware to millions. The cost of buying the program will be only five dollars. You estimate that 50,000 internet users will take you up on the offer in the first year.

Now you estimate the cost of purchasing equipment, postage, printing, insurance, internet access, and the like for the first year. When you finish your calculation you discover that your annual income in profits will be around $10,000. Currently you make $80,000 as an IS manager. Thus, the math tells you to keep the day job.

If, on the other hand, you meet someone from another software company that says they are willing to market your new product for $49 a copy at stores everywhere, while paying you 10% royalties, the math may change. You may discover a potential to make $250,000 the first year.

The only way to know where your stand is to perform a realistic analysis of your idea. This is done by drawing up a business plan. Instructions for doing this are located in your local library, chamber of commerce, and of course, on the internet. By going through these steps you get a good idea of what will be involved in becoming an internet success story. At the same time, you will have a document to show to investment bankers, venture capitalists, corporate attorneys, and accountants. They will be more than happy to show you the holes in your plans. The exercise will result in a very realistic view of your idea. Decision-making from that point should be fairly easy.

Internal Spin-Off

If, in contrast, your staff has an idea for a new product or service for the internet that has very large potential, you may want to create an internal spin-off. This is where a part of the department is separated to work on this special project. Only the best people are put on the project and frequently outside experts are brought in to consult. At the same time, management is keeping a close eye on activities. Your personnel assigned to the project realize that success means recognition and a good paragraph for any resume.

We have to look at the process of the search for venture capital in two separate lights. First, the seeking of private funds for a new business start-up takes us through several difficult steps where the project has to be repeatedly justified to skeptical outsiders. Second, this same process can be used internally in a slightly less harsh version to encourage your own personnel to think through each project carefully. If a project can not be justified by these means then why are you implementing it?

At the same time, this type of activities promotes higher morale among IS staff. Having to build a business plan and then justify it several times is a challenge. People will rise to a challenge. Especially when they realize that this is preparing them with the skills needed to promote themselves in the outside world. Naturally, we are taking a chance that these same staff members might leave your company to start their own businesses. However, you can build relationships with the companies they create so that you continue to benefit from the skills you teach them.

When you face a shortage of skilled people in the IS department, one method of correcting the problem is to join forces with the teams that have the people you need. In the previous example, you developed IS staff members now capable of forming their own companies through careful business planning. You can also invest directly into promising contracting businesses that provide talented IS staff members. Resources can be shared between your company and the contracting house. They may need graphic artists and you may need Oracle experts.

More on the Business Plan

Please keep in mind that we are describing the use of a business plan and venture capital as a model you can copy for internal use or for striking out on your own. The key ingredients in a successful internet-related company are:

- effective management
- adequate capital
- a solid plan
- realistic projections of growth
- enough resources to get the job done

This all has to be put into place and managed successfully before a competitor beats you to the market.

In our example, we are trying to build a streaming media channel of training videos and courses. The internet will be used as the primary delivery system. This could just as easily be a corporate project where the IS department is setting up the same system for broadcast over the intranet used by your company.

In either case you need to justify what you are doing to several people that will be very skeptical. For example, in the venture capital world this means convincing not only investors, but hired managers, staff, bankers, and possible content suppliers that you are for real and your idea is sound. In the corporate world you will have to convince the human relations director, the VP of finance, the training manager, and your own staff that this can be carried out to the benefit of the company.

There is nothing worse than getting an idea implemented only to discover that it is causing more problems than it solves. In the case of seeking venture capital you need to list out the potential risks and how you plan to avoid them as part of your business plan.

Returning to our example, we have put together a pretty good idea of how we want the service structured. We know that we want a lot of streaming video content for the internet. This is usually the point where most IS managers make the big mistake. Specifically, they let the software and hardware seduce them from good planning. At this point it would be easy to start shopping for video streaming servers, backend software for controlling the pay-per-view aspect of the project, and web site locations.

This would not be the proper first move. Instead, you need to sit down and start doing some financial calculations. How much will it cost to digitized each video tape per minute? What will be the staffing costs? How much more floor space is needed? What are the costs of insurance, phones, internet connections, benefits, and the like? This all has to be placed into a business model that can tell you the day to day expenses of running such a service. Then you must estimate the revenue that the project might generate. Between these two figures you come up with break even points and time until profitability.

Armed with the business model for the cash required, you now seek out more efficient ways of providing the services. You might start by approaching a major training video library owner and asking for a joint partnership. This allows you to obtain the tapes and perhaps their conversion into a digital form at a lower cost. Is it low enough to warrant the partnership?

Perhaps you discover that a major internet portal, such as America Online, wants a training channel on its broadband services. Or, perhaps one of the DSL services wants your service to help justify their DSL subscriptions to potential business customers. Either way you might find that you can reduce expenses. For example, perhaps your new partner already has extensive video streaming capabilities and software for tracking customers. This makes your time to market much quicker while holding down costs.

Such relationships also help to encourage investors to place money into your hands. They are looking for companies that are well-placed with interesting technologies and a high probability of going public or being bought out at a great profit.

This means that you have to build relationships, whether this is an internal project or a venture capital project. Part of this building is finding a person to run the business. For internal projects, that means looking through your current staff for who is a good organizer. Don't stay within just your staff—also look at other managers within the company. Make it clear to your staff that this is a high-visibility position that they have to compete for. This further promotes a strong team within the IS department. For outside venture capital projects, this means looking for an established name in the field. For example, the recently retired president of a streaming video company.

The people placed in charge of your project will free you up for your job as IS manager. These people will also lend credibility to the project, whether internal or external. This, in turn, tends to promote more of the relationships you need to make the project a success.

The people you choose also have to have expertise in the matter at hand. In the business plan (and later the investment memorandum), you need these talents to demonstrate you have the brain power and intellectual property to complete the task and to complete it well. The right mixture of personalities and talents will also inspire the staff members on such a venture. The result is a greater probability of success.

We should also pause at this point to discuss the matter of legality. In a venture capital project like we are describing here you would have an attorney for contractual matters, another for intellectual property issues, and one more for security transactions. In the public world these lawyers are valuable members of your team. They keep you from making serious legal mistakes that can quickly sink an otherwise sound idea.

Internally, you have to use the legal department in a similar way. Take the case of a domain name for your new project. You may discover that the name you want to use is already taken by an outside company. Using a very similar name could lead to confusion or worse. Another pitfall to avoid is the failure to do a trademark search on your idea. You may reach market just in time to discover that another company has an almost identical product and they are now sending a letter telling you to "ceases and desist."

Finally, you have to sit down and think about how your product will be different from anything else that is already available. That means a complete search for any software or hardware solutions that can also solve the problem you are addressing. If such products exist, you have to justify the cost of developing your idea versus purchasing the other product.

For example, you may want to build a streaming media server application, but several streaming media servers are already on the market. For a venture capital project you would have to build a strong enough case to convince potential investors that your product is so much better or revolutionary that customers will flock in to buy. The same holds true for internal projects. Many times IS departments fail to take any action because they simply cannot decide on whether to develop a new application or to buy an existing application. Instead of setting up a rigorous system of justifying the self-development, they linger for months afraid to hurting someone's feelings. By using the method we are describing, you avoid this and also make the proposing groups feel much more confident with their idea. At the same time, management gets a clear picture of the benefits and risks from the decision to be made.

Finally, we put all of this information together to form the business plan. From that will come the investment memorandum for the venture capital team, or the business case for the internal team.

Creating the Business Plan

As mentioned earlier, the use of a formal business plan is good for startup companies and it can build moral internally by making the staff justify their decisions on major projects. By making a presentation to senior management the staff has to buy into the project and show confidence.

Business plans are typically 40 to 50 pages in length as a minimum. They are made up of the number of sections. Each section has its own particular purpose. In general, a business plan has the following:

- Statement of Confidentiality
- Executive Summary
- Mission Statement
- Present Status
- Description of Product or Service
- Target Markets
- Marketing and Sales Strategies
- Development Plans
- Management Team
- Financial Projections
- Funding Requirement
- Timing
- Conclusion
- Appendices

We will examine each of the sections in detail to see what type content to add. Working through each of the sections should give you the clear idea on the strength of your proposed venture.

Statement of confidentiality

This would be used only for outside groups starting their own company. This is a statement that the information contained in the document is confidential and should not be shared with others. When seeking venture capital you will have to present the business plan to several groups and individuals. This statement is the beginning of making sure that others do not take your idea and form their own company.

Executive summary

The executive summary is the portion of the business plan that will be sent to potential investors or senior managers. It is an overview of the proposed project or new product. It should highlight the need for the new product or service. It should introduce the team working on the project and a very brief overview of their qualifications.

The executive summary for venture capital should mention the amount of money being asked for and how much ownership comes with shares of the company. This type of language is best left for investment bankers and securities attorneys.

It should also discuss why the new product or service is needed, who is the potential customer, and why these customers would demand such a product or service. The idea is to make a quick and convincing argument for your venture. A good summary will invite a fast request for the full business plan.

Mission statement

In the main volume we spent a good deal of time discussing the need for a mission statement for the IS department that is supported by policies and procedures. The connection between these documents and the business plan is made here for internal projects. It allows you to show why the proposed project would help complete the department's or the company's strategic goals.

For an outside venture, you would state a mission statement for the new company and outline the strategic objectives of the new company. In addition, you would discuss penetration of the target market, quality assurance system, management team, and any other relevant pieces of information.

Present status

For both internal and external ventures you have to discuss your current status. The mission statement tells the reader where you are going. The status portion of the business plan tells the reader where you are starting from. In the case of an external venture you usually have invested your own money or already have seed money to get the new company started. These should be described.

For internal projects, you discuss the current funding available in your budget for this project and the additional amount you will need. You also discuss the resources your currently have and the additional resources that will be required. This gives senior management a good picture of what it will take to initiate the project. The actual description of how you get to your objectives comes later in the plan.

Description of product or service

The new product or service should be described in detail. This would include the features of the new product or service that makes it unique. In short, you have to convince other people that your approach to a problem is so much better than anything else that customers will flock towards it. Part of this description would be a discussion of the current environment. This would include competing products and alternative solutions.

The idea is to draw a fair and accurate picture of the world as far as this product or service is concerned. In our example we are talking about streaming training videos. At the current time just about any training company of any size is looking into delivering this same service. However, the approach is scattered and unorganized. Each is selecting their own compression format and method of viewing the video. This is quickly leading to a confusing array of methods for the average customer. The customer needs to have MicroSoft Media Play, Real Audio's G2, and several proprietary viewers on their system to see the training videos from several sources.

In contrast, our proposal is for standardizing all videos to the Media Player and using a major portal (i.e., Yahoo, AOL, Lycos, etc.) to sponsor a Training Channel for broadband customers. This portal would be open to all training companies, but the interface used would be the one we develop. The results would be less confusion for the customer and more choices at a single location. In fact, a search engine could be used to look for the topic required by the customer.

Target markets

The hardest part about a business plan is accurately guessing the reception of your new product or service by a particular target market. Usually, naming the target markets is fairly straight-forward. You stick to the obvious choices.

In our example, you talk about the small and medium-sized companies that need to have a low, fixed training budget and how the new streaming training videos can meet that need.

The number of such companies is available in demographic information. The tough part is guessing how many of these companies will sign up for your new service. Ten percent market penetration is considered excellent for most ventures. Therefore, if you find that there are just over 600,000 companies in your target market, then a two percent penetration would represent 12,000 customers within one year. Such numbers are used to plan for growth.

However, most internet technologies tend to find their way into unexpected markets. For example, screen savers were expected to be simple ways to keep your monitor image fresh. The SETI at Home project used a new screen saver to tap into the unused time on individual computers to analyze data from the radio search for extraterrestrial life. Almost two million users signed up to help. Suddenly, the market for screen savers grew unexpectedly.

If you can anticipate such possibilities, just list them. Leave them out of your business plan. Instead use them for contingency planning. For example, you might be aware that colleges would want to tap into your library of training videos. Likewise, individuals may want to view the videos. Potentially, your demand for viewing could be two to five times higher than you are planning. Someone should take the time to calculate how to scale up your resources to meet such a demand. Then if the demand does suddenly grow, you are prepared.

Marketing and sales strategies

Good products and services usually don't sell themselves. It requires a marketing and sales effort for both internal and external projects to get the new service or product used by the customers. Internally, this usually means a roll-out with training and orientation. Externally, it means hiring a sales and marketing force to first raise customer awareness and then get the customers to part with some of their money.

Either way, you have to know the appealing features and limitations of the product or service you are brining to market. You need to exploit the competitive advantages of the product while answering concerns about possible limitations. Careful thinking in this area can result in a successful project.

Development plans

Here is where you actually detail the project management approach and schedule for the new product or service. In our example there are going to be many steps between start of the project and a point we will call "successful conclusion." Video tape rights have to be obtained, encoding equipment purchased, software written, databases created, and the like.

In an external venture, investors want to see a working version of the software, or better still, a list of current customers using the service. Investors are looking for a good idea that is just taking off and has a lot of potential, while controlling a good share of the market. Internally, the senior management team is looking for good ideas with a good return on the investment, a way to make current customers happy, and a way to obtain additional customers.

In most cases, you cannot fulfill all of these desires. It is best to fulfill as many as possible. If you cannot, then you should rethink the entire venture. Without obvious benefits and a positive cash flow, you have to do a lot more justification.

Management team

Critical to both internal and external projects is the strength of the management team. Venture capitalists and private investors look at this first. They want to see seasoned and highly experienced managers leading the company. This is why you see so many Fortune 500 executives being lured away to internet startup companies. A good manager that is well-known is worth the price because it almost always buys you investors.

The same can be said about internal projects. The senior management team will look to see if well-known and dependable managers with a record of success are backing the project. If not, they see nothing but trouble ahead. This is why you describe the qualifications of each manager for this project and include a resume.

Financial projections

The earnings potential of the project is summarized here. This is where you want to make solid financial projections. For example, our example project anticipates 12,000 companies signing up for the video services at an average subscription cost of $345 per company. That should generate $4.14 million dollars of income. This has to be contrasted against the nearly one million dollar cost of developing the support software and the two million dollars spent on staff, encoding, and other expenses. The result is a clear profit margin.

You would also project a worse case and best case model of income and expenses. This should show that the company is fairly sure to stay in business for a few years.

Funding requirement

The results of your projection work is a clear statement of how much funding you require to proceed. Typically, you try to get two to three years of funding. You also need to discuss when you will break even and no longer need funding. You must state your funding needs clearly. For example, if it takes 10 million dollars to launch and sustain the video project, ask for 10 million dollars.

Underfunding is one of the chief reasons venture companies fail—the management team is too shy to ask for enough money. In reality, many venture capitalists today will not bother with any request for two million dollars or less.

Timing

Next you must discuss timing. When do you need the money? The best approach for you is to get all of the money up front. That way you do not need to spend additional time in the future re-justifying your project. Also, you won't get cut off from funding just when you need the money.

Conclusion

Finally, you finish with an overall conclusion. Basically, you are saying that your idea is superior, customers will love it, the company will benefit, money is to be made, and we need to get started right now. This is your chance to close the deal. Just like we discussed in the e-commerce chapters, many companies fail because they are too shy to ask for a closure with a customer. In a business plan you must finish with strength and confidence. The numbers must support your argument and the argument must be reasonable.

Appendices

You can use appendices to add additional material, such as resumes, example screens from the software, letters of intent, memorandums of understanding, and the like. The idea is to show depth in your argument. If you say you have a strong management team, show the resumes that demonstrate this. If you say you have several major customers and more that want to sign up, list the existing customers and reprint any letters of intent.

Chapter S6
Implementing Wireless, Bots, and Other New Technologies

Nokia expects that by the end of 2003 there will be 500 million PCs in the world. They believe that there will be 600 million net-enabled handsets by the end of 2003. What does this mean to you as an IS manager?

Let's just say that Nokia is overly optimistic and that there will be 600 million net-enabled handsets at the end of 2004 instead 2003. That means that almost all IS organizations will have an established infrastructure and management system to deal with wireless handsets in 2003. The system will have to be just as complete as all the management systems in place for LAN-based PCs now. Trained technicians, help desk support, and asset management processes to procure, secure, track, and dispose of the things, will have to be fully established and working by the end of 2003.

There will be no competitive advantage to not having a good wireless management system in place. You will be out of business if you do not. Businesses that need to maintain a competitive advantage in their field will have had the whole thing in place by 2002 in order to maintain their position.

That means that by the end of 2001, a competitive business must have an IS manager who has completed the planning, design, and testing of a strong wireless infrastructure with pilot sites humming along. Now, what if Nokia is not overly optimistic and each phase has to be completed one year earlier?

Managing at Internet Speeds

The Internet has expanded so quickly into the business world with such explosive growth that many information technology specialists are finding themselves in IS management positions without a lot of management experience. If you are in such a position there are some good ideas to help you get started.

Create a vision

People love to work toward a definite goal that is important and that challenges them. IS people are no exception. If you are a leader in IS, it is your responsibility to look at the work that needs to be done in the next two years and find the most important elements. Simplify those elements into something clear, meaningful and important. If there is no challenging and meaningful work to be done, get another job. If you are good at managing information systems, you will find work somewhere else with no great effort. As a manager, creating the vision is the single most important responsibility.

Communicate the vision

Of course you know this already. But did you know that almost no one does it very well? After many years of management experience I would say that the best IS managers communicate about 30 to 40% of what they should to employees, customers, bosses etc. I do not know why but I have seen IS managers get caught up in the daily activity of getting the job done and not telling people what they need to know. Learn to communicate 50% as much as you should and you will be successful beyond your wildest dreams.

How to Set Goals

If you are going to be able to manage at Internet speeds you are going to have to be able to manage some things the old way. Some things just work, and goal-setting principles have been understood for a long time. Make your goals specific, measurable, aggressive, and reachable.

- *Specific*—Please do not ever confuse making the goal specific with making how to do it specific. If you have spent most of your career excelling at doing computer stuff, managing could be a difficult transition for you. This is similar to excellent athletes becoming managers of other athletes. They are rarely successful because it is such a difficult transition. Resist the temptation to show people how to get their jobs done. People like to succeed. They will find their own way to do it but you must make the goals specific. Vague goals never give the thrill of victory.

- *Measurable*—I never did believe the cliché that you cannot manage what you cannot measure but I still agree that you should make your goals measurable. Just figuring out how you should measure progress toward meeting the goals will give you great insight into what you are actually trying to get done.

- *Aggressive*—Engaged, enthusiastic, and challenged people can accomplish amazing things. If you keep your goals aggressive, the best people will be attracted to your organization and good people will tend to stay longer.

- *Reachable*—Some extraordinary leaders may set goals that appear to most people as unreachable. There are also some people who have succeed by setting goals beyond what can be reached in order to stretch people's abilities to the maximum. Neither of these methods can be sustained. As long as your goals are aggressive being reachable will not become a limitation.

Here is something else that works—subdivide your project into two-month periods with weekly deliverables. Just be sure the deliverables are specific, measurable, aggressive and reachable.

- *Give people responsibility and power.* This is extraordinarily difficult, especially for people like you who are competent and self confident and successful. Every time you tell people what to do instead of what must be accomplished you limit what they can accomplish. In order to tell people what to do, you have to think very carefully about how it should be accomplished and dozens of other details that they can work out on their own. This takes away from the time you should spend on creating and communicating a vision and watching what is really going on in your organization.

- *Organize once and leave it alone.* Reorganizing gives the appearance of doing something important but it is mostly activity with not much in the way of results. If you have an organization that is working leave it alone. If you are starting with a new organization or have to reorganize for some reason there is a powerful way to organize for IS management which I first learned from the Gartner Group.

One reason it is so powerful is that it deals so well with the fact that everything is always in a state of transition. Intellectually, people can see that things are always changing but emotionally, most IS shops feel that once they get through this big project things will get back to normal and they will begin to get some real work done. That is how they organize and that is how they work, always as if they were just about to get back to normal. It never happens.

Normal is change. Normal is constant transition to a new way of working with no let up. Your organizational structure should recognize that. It should be designed around constant change and should provide the stability that makes change fun rather than exhausting.

Achieving Goals

Four functions that an IS group should perform to go about achieving its goals are planning, design, implementation and operations.

Planning

The most important function is planning and it is the least likely group that you will be able to form in your organization. First of all, very few computer people can stand to plan anything. They love to react, they love to investigate, they love to solve difficult problems and they love to experiment. You absolutely must find at least one person to put on the planning team. More are orders of magnitude better but people with planning skills will be extremely difficult to find. They have to understand technology. They have to see the big picture from a business perspective. They have to read obsessively. They have to be able to talk to people at every level in the organization. They have to be bold. They have to have an uncommon amount of common sense.

If you do find people who can plan, be careful. The next higher level in your organization will absolutely freak out when they hear you have a planning group. "You do not understand. I do the planning. You carry out the plans. We cannot have dozens of different plans being made." It is amazing that so many otherwise brilliant people can fail to grasp the fact that planning must take place at every level. Of course you take the organization's plan as your starting point but failure to plan carefully and formally at each level disrupts unity more than it preserves unity.

At the first sign of resistance, give up. Rename the planning team "Facilitation" or "Acquisition" or "Cost Reduction." Just be sure that they know they are the planning team and that the design team knows they are the planners. No one else absolutely has to know except you.

Design

The second team is responsible for design. After the first team makes a plan, the design team has to study it and agree that they can design a solution that accomplishes the goals of the plan. Make them put it in writing. More about this later but it should be very, very formal.

The design team works out exactly what kind by brand name and model, how many, when, installed and operated by how many people, where, how much it will cost and what specifications it will be measured by. They are also in charge of testing and certification. If you have programmers, they are on the design team. When they are finished they have a product in writing that can be handed over to the installation team.

Implementation

The implementation team examines the design and says, "Yes, we can put that in place." Otherwise, they give it back to design for further work. The implementation team manages the procurement, project management, training and installation of the system or application.

Operations

When the system is in place and working everywhere with no need for significant modifications, the operations team accepts responsibility for operating and maintaining the system or application including help desk and ongoing training. Make them examine the system and agree in writing that it is in place and working before they sign for it.

Now, put a different person in charge of following each project through the entire process. Have these people report to you every week with the status of the project and expected completion dates. The team leaders are really managing the project through each phase, but someone needs to feel ownership of the project and to be sure it does not get lost or delayed.

Here is an example of how this succeeded for me (and where I failed) a couple of years ago:

The problem   An information technology department I managed decided to undertake an organizational reengineering initiative. The organization had recently gone through a high-profile, very successful client-server and network infrastructure implementation. This brought recognition from higher headquarters and a large increase in new projects.

The driver for reorganization was frustration and burnout on the part of IS staff when the workload and complexity of projects began to rise quickly. Although this was a strong department with recognized successes, the number of late projects and dropped assignments was beginning to grow.

Due to their strong technical and management abilities, the most capable computer specialists were being assigned far more projects than they could handle. The other technicians had fewer projects, but often ran into difficulty with complex technical problems. It was not easy for them to get help from the overworked experts. Management found tracking of projects difficult because the technicians could not take time for routine reports and avoided meetings that involved long discussions about projects that did not pertain to them directly. Most of the discussions would have been of some value but in the difficult situation they preferred to use their time working on their specific project problems.

The approach   Off-site meetings were held to devise a plan to cope with the increasing complexity. There was a strong group confidence because of the record of success but a high level of stress because of the increasing problems with project management. In spite of the solid, shared values of the group, there was sharp disagreement about how to solve the problem. One group felt that a team approach was necessary to provide technicians the mutual support needed to accomplish the heavier workload. The other group worried that dividing project tasks between teams would limit accountability and continuity as well as create bottlenecks. They wanted an individual project manager to work each project.

A consensus was reached to divide the IS directorate into four teams—planning, design, implementation, and operations. Each team would take responsibility for one of those four aspects of every project. To assure continuity of project management, it was agreed that one person, who could be drawn from any of the four teams, would be given responsibility to be the point of contact for each project. That solution removed the pressure of a single person taking on the entire workload of a project since the teams would do the work together. At the same time, there would always be a specific person who could report on the status of a project and personally keep that project moving through the process even if new projects with higher visibility were added to the workload.

In effect, the structure became the strategy. With the structure decided on, the team moved on to create a system to institutionalize the procedures, processes, and routines necessary to guide and track the workload and to assign resources in the most effective way.

The leadership and key members of the organization saw the need for fundamental change. There was no external organization bringing pressure to take action. Therefore the tasks were approached somewhat informally. The list of tasks likely to be included in a fundamental change effort suggested by Beckhard and Pritchard[1] includes:

- A detailed study of the present conditions
- Collection of data on the attitudes of the organization's members toward the change
- Creation of models of the desired state

[1] Beckhard, R., and Pritchard, W. A. *Changing the Essence: The Art of Creating and Leading Fundamental Change in Organizations,* 1992, p. 70.

- Identification of and planning for a transitional management
- Assignment of functions to the transitional management
- A formal statement of the change goals and a clear description of the end state
- Identification and allocation of dedicated resources, experts, and consultants

Each of these tasks either received sufficient attention or proved to be unnecessary for this effort with one significant exception. A formal statement of the change goals and a clear description of the end state was not implemented. Adverse consequences of that oversight are addressed in following sections.

The system   The group developed the following system:

- A planning team would define the mission requirements of each incoming project and coordinate priorities and budget requirements with the IS director. This would also be coordinated with the functional business office that would use the completed system or application. The planning team defined the broad outlines of the types of hardware, software and processes to be used. They also determined the overall timeframes and other critical parameters of the project.
- The design team accepted the plan and used it to design a specific solution to the problem or project and created a detailed timetable by site. In addition to specifications and standards, the design team designated resources and included them in the timetables. The design team would also be responsible for devising a training plan for each project.
- The implementation team accepted the design, purchased the equipment and installed the hardware in the field with the help of the LAN administrators who would support the system.
- The operations team would accept the installed system upon evidence that it was fully tested, functional and documented. They would operate and maintain the system until it was significantly changed.

The analysis   The structure as strategy approach was good in that the organization benefited from the improved alignments. The team leaders made much better use of resources than had been possible with the centralized control of the director. However, in spite of these improvements, the strategy was weaker than it might have been. The strategic plan was not carefully thought out and was never formally announced and advertised throughout the IS department or to the business units of the organization. For these reasons the strategy did not become a unifying principle and alignment was less than it might have been. Because there were strong shared values among the team leaders, the IS organization retained its strong momentum and continued to produce at a high level. However, the participation and alignment of the lower-level technicians may have been raised with a clear-cut and better-advertised strategy.

The structure (planning, design, implementations, and operations) has remained a strong and effective aspect of the organization. The structure contributed to the establishment of fairly small, self-managing teams capable of quick and adaptable response in the face of changes. The structure had very positive symbolic value to the organization in that it delivered an image of professionalism and order which not only maintained a strong sense of camaraderie but also kept people focused on critical aspects of the IS mission. Just looking at the organization chart was a reminder that the goal of implementing operational programs would be achieved through careful planning and design. The structure also contributed to the establishment of effective processes within the organization. The procedures and routines necessary to deliver good results were guided by the new structure. Without continual emphasis, both planning and design get neglected when organizations are under severe time restraints. Under those conditions, IS organizations become reactive rather than proactive. Events beyond its control may overwhelm a reactive organization.

The procedures and routines affected by the reengineering were effective but could have been better. The original plan of having a formal, signed transfer of each project from team to team was never enforced. Handoffs soon became very informal and then gradually began to lose visibility altogether. The results were not catastrophic, but there were occasional lapses and priority conflicts. Small projects often got short shrift and failed to go through the official planning, design, and implementation phases. Occasionally, minor projects were dropped until headquarters or functional departments asked for status. Lack of discipline, rather than weakness in the reengineering may have contributed most to this problem, however; there was nothing built into the structure to keep this key process in focus. A more formal report of project movement through each phase would have been more effective.

The strength of the organization both before and after the reengineering was primarily due to the unusually high skill level of the top technicians. The reengineering effort multiplied the effectiveness of the strongest technicians. It also raised both the effectiveness and the skill level of the journeyman technicians who now had strong teams to guide them as well as more access to the most highly skilled technicians. Before the reorganization, the best technicians were taking the hardest projects from start to completion regardless of the skill level required for the component tasks of the project. After the reengineering, the best technicians could take on the hardest, and therefore to them, the best tasks, but could still assist other technicians in getting through the problems they were facing. The new structure made much more effective use of the skills within the organization.

Conclusion   In terms of overall outcomes, the re-engineering was very successful. Accountability was improved because the progress of projects was better tracked as they were moved from team to team. Focus on operational systems and infrastructure was improved because the structure of the organization pointed to operational results. However, as noted, once the novelty of the new system wore off, the formal handing off of projects from team to team degenerated into informal, individual tracking of the minor projects and dropped assignments have increased to some degree.

The structure was organized around desired outcomes, which did result in more seamless, customized customer service. The self-managing teams proved to be an effective means of moving downstream information upstream. The improved alignment encouraged the journeyman technicians to take on more difficult projects without fear because they knew they had the teams to support them through each phase of their projects.

The "form follows function" strategy of separate, self-managing teams to perform planning, design, implementation and operations functions was very effective in aligning the IS department to the goals of supporting the business. The clear and unifying vision provided an effective and supportive work atmosphere. Lack of a formal, disciplined ritual of moving projects between teams reduced the effectiveness of the re-engineering effort. The lack of a formal and clear description of the End State very likely contributed to this situation.

Your Network Architecture over the Internet

Virtual private networks

When you have remote offices with large amounts of traffic to the main office, it often pays to lease dedicated circuits between the two locations. That way you get high-speed access and excellent security. However, you also get a bill of several hundred to several thousand dollars per month as well.

When you do not have the high-speed requirements to justify a leased circuit, dial access has been the usual solution. But dial access is expensive, has security problems, and requires the additional expense of setting up and maintaining modem pools. With the advent of the internet, virtual private networks (VPNs) has provided another solution.

With a VPN provider, your remote office can dial a local Internet Service Provider to reduce dial costs. The data is encrypted at the PC (or at the VPN provider) and decrypted at your central office site. This provides potential cost savings and security. VPN technology has been just about to explode in use every year for the past three or four years but has not reached its potential for several reasons.

You need a big provider of VPN services. Some of the good providers have not yet reached the size needed to provide nationwide service. Many businesses that need VPN need dial access because they have people scattered widely around the country. A state or regional service provider cannot offer service in enough places to attract large customers. If you have users in many locations you have to look at the big providers.

You will not be satisfied with complex, difficult or clunky security. Only easy security will keep your people dialing in and getting their work done efficiently. The need for easy security applies not only to the client portion of your VPN but to the network management portion as well. If you have to assign many of your highly skilled people to managing and maintaining the security, the price rises very quickly. Unfortunately, easy security does not really exist yet. You can only hope for degrees of improvement available only from the very best providers.

Effective security is obviously even more critical than easy security. Right now, with the absence of any permanently secure system, you have to look for a flexible and scalable security system for your VPN network. You need a VPN provider that can help you stay a few steps ahead of the vandals and spies intent on damaging your business. Effective security is achieved generally with options for encryption, PC firewalls, and authentication and access control.

There are many components in any dial system and this makes it very difficult to provide a dependable service. The technology has not quite matured to the degree that you can risk your business on consistent availability from any vendor. There are simply too many points of failure in any large-scale dial operation. At the client end, there are many different configurations of software and hardware. This makes it very difficult for any VPN provider to be flexible enough to serve huge numbers of different customers. These customers are also dialing through a very undependable phone system in many cases. Some of the dial users are located in areas of the country with phone service that is fine for voice but inadequate for data.

You need reasonable speed. With a VPN you are creating packets of data at the remote PC. The packets are encrypted and then wrapped in an IP packet. This is called IP tunneling because in a way remote users are tunneling through the Internet inside of IP packets to get to your main site. The packets are unwrapped on the receiving end. The IP tunneling requires some overhead and therefore reduces the overall communications speed which wasn't that fast to begin with.

The speed drag of encrypting your packets is even worse. This is called a VPN because you are using the Internet but virtually creating a private network. The promise is that you will have the cheap access of the Internet and the security and speed of traffic passing over your own private network. The reality is that the tunneling and encryption take time.

In spite of all these problems, the best providers are beginning to significantly improve the quality of service available. And, you may need VPN enough to accept some of the problems while the service gets closer to being what you would prefer. VPN technology and the service level providers are now beginning to deliver is improving significantly.

The key is to look at VPN not as a technology that is good or bad but as a tool that is or is not worth the money. Remember the problem areas listed above. When you go shopping for VPN capability you will have to pay cold hard cash to avoid each of them. All of the problems can be solved they just cost money.

Now, get with the business people in your company. Determine the benefit of a VPN. That will not be easy. The benefits or costs of things like faster or slower access is not easy to quantify. That is not the most difficult analysis though. You and the business people will also have to determine the benefits of improved security. Everyone agrees more security is better but it is excruciatingly difficult to determine just exactly how many dollars better. Get used to it. If you go through the work of quantifying the benefits of faster service and better security you will use that information again and again and again. What is even more important is that you, unlike 90% of the IS people in the world, will be aligning technology to the business. That will be critical to the survival and profitability of your company.

After you find a VPN provider big enough with relatively easy, yet strong security and with dependable, fast enough service to make the cost and effort worthwhile, here are a few things you also need to consider:

Pay for a system with fail-over capability. By that I mean a system with redundant equipment on your premises that automatically passes the traffic from a failed system to the good one. If you have been managing dial access through a modem pool at your main office you may have grown a little complacent if terms of reliability. If one or two or five people have trouble dialing into your system, well you are busy with LANs and WANs and web sites, etc. Unless it is the boss having problems the dial system may not have highest priority for resources.

With a VPN you may have hundreds or thousands of people coming into your site through one piece of hardware. Failure there gets expensive quickly. Buy the automatic fail-over option as a high priority unless you can afford system failure for long periods of time.

If you have a large enough system to warrant more than one piece of hardware, look long and hard at the load balancing option. The people accessing your system will change their work patterns every time there is a business or an application change. Load balancing will greatly decrease the likelihood of mysterious slowdowns causing problems that are difficult to duplicate.

Be sure to monitor performance. Ideally, start monitoring before you implement a VPN system. A baseline will not only vastly improve your ability to see the affect of the VPN on your current system, it will provide you with vital information for determining the type and size of VPN solution you need to buy. The kinds of things you need to baseline and monitor are availability, response time, and throughput.

Be conservative. Do not believe the sales people's claims about performance. Their claims are the somewhat exaggerated results of tests on a closed track using professional drivers on a sunny day. Your benchmarking should give you some clues about where the performance bottlenecks will occur. Talk about those to the business people before you buy. That way, when the complaints about speed come rolling in, and they will, the business people will not feel betrayed. They will nod wisely at the complainers and say, "Yes well, we considered the R315-Z, but the payback just did not warrant the additional investment." You have just avoided a helpdesk call and an uncomfortable staff meeting. Business/technology alignment is grand.

Be prepared for lots of problems. No one is running the crazy mix of legacy and home-brewed software programs you are using. Some of them are using protocols that are not considered standard by the people who invented your VPN system. When people use your VPN they will assume that they are going to get gigabit performance 24 hours a day. Manage expectations while avoiding undue pessimism.

Security over the Internet

The best way to secure your web-based data is a well-planned architecture. And a well-planned security system will provide multi-layered defenses and improve response time to your web pages.

Start with basic database management practices such as putting data and data applications in different file locations, and even different physical machines wherever possible. This is more difficult to control than you might think, however. Small workgroups create local applications that improve efficiency, then other workgroups borrow the application, and soon there's pressure to make it an official enterprise application. After all, it works great (locally) and it is free! Well, it isn't free. Experience shows it will take significant funding to create enterprise applications with appropriate security, scalability and maintenance. It may be a good idea to convert the application, but it will be lots of work, or worse, a huge disaster with security holes, application crashes, and poor documentation. Create an organizational law forbidding the move of any application beyond a local workgroup without being redesigned for the enterprise. Get the approval of the boss on this law before it becomes an issue.

Keeping data on a separate machine allows you to put in strong controls. No computer can look at or change the data except the application server. This may not stop the dedicated professional, who may be able to spoof the machine names, but it certainly keeps out the riff raff.

Next step, make sure that no one, not even a user, can access the web application server. How do you do that? Create a proxy server. Again, make this a separate physical machine if at all possible. Only the proxy server can access the application server, while the proxy server takes requests from users and passes them on to the applications server, which is the only machine allowed access to the data. This greatly increases your security.

The second advantage to the proxy server is caching web pages and other data. The first person who requests data waits while the proxy server makes it's own request to the applications server, then the proxy sends data on to the user. Time consuming, but usually necessary. The second person requesting the same web page or data gets it straight from the proxy server's cache. Instant gratification!

"Usually" necessary for the first data request? Not always? There are two kinds of cache: cache on demand, and cache on command. Cache on demand is what we have just described. The proxy server puts the commonly demanded data into memory, reducing access times just where you need them most—for the data most people are requesting.

Cache on command sets up a list of files that will always reside in high-speed memory. During the night, if that is when your workload is lightest, the files with daily updates will be loaded into proxy server memory. You'll need a lot of memory, but memory is cheaper than payroll.

The Directory server is the heart of the whole system. When a user is allowed through your firewall to a web server a message goes immediately to the directory server saying, "Who is this guy?" The directory server has all the user identification and access rights information you need in one spot. User information can include whatever you need including phone numbers, passwords, access rights for applications and specific data within applications. This server can make your Internet web server system immensely powerful. It provides pinpoint control and wide availability in one package.

The directory lets you have a secure Intranet for your own company while at the same time allowing other companies access to data inside your system on a selective basis to particular pieces of information.

The Tools and Applications Running the Internet Today

Public key infrastructure (PKI)

Once you understand public and private keys, everything else in PKI is market share and management detail. Well, there is also the math but you do not need to understand that any more than you need to know how to design a memory chip. You already know that longer keys are generally more secure than shorter keys and slower to encrypt and decrypt.

Single Key encryption uses a single binary number to both encrypt and decrypt data. Security is pretty much a function of how long you make the number and how much you trust that the secret is safe with the other key holder. Encryption and decryption is fast, however; as the number of people communicating increases, the number of keys required becomes too large to manage easily. If there are five people you need 10 keys, 50 people need 2,450 and 10,000 people need close to 50 million.

Public Key encryption uses two keys. One key (public key) can encrypt messages but cannot be used to decrypt the message. The other key can decrypt the message (private key). This system has tremendous potential for use on the internet. Provide all of your customers with your public key. Now they can send you orders or financial information that only you can read. Or, you can send your public key to all of your remote offices, which can then safely send reports to your headquarters.

Public key technology can be used by large numbers of people but is very slow. Single key is fast so in practice, encryption of the message is done with single key technology. The single decrypt key is then encrypted using public key technology. Now slow public key only has to decrypt one word—the Private Key—which is then used to decrypt the message quickly. This provides the best advantages of each system.

The management issues of public key technology require an infrastructure of institutions and trust relationships to work properly. You need to manage the authentication, encryption, and secure directory services of your web architecture. This is handled by means of certificate authority. The problems involved with managing certificate authority are what have held up the wide spread adoption of PKI all these years.

It is all very comforting to know that the public key encrypted message can only be read by the sender. But what do you do when you get a message saying, "Please send all your plans for your new expansion project using this handy public key," love, Your Bank? Is it really the bank? The message better be signed and notarized. That is what a certificate authority does. A third party vouches for the authenticity of the sender and binds a digital signature to the public key. Where stronger security is needed, smart cards containing the keys are distributed in person to each user by trusted security people. The smart cards require a password and or a biometric security device in order to be used.

Once you have your organizational PKI designed you can use a set of servers to manage the system. Once you get your system of servers running you will call that your PKI but do not forget that it is the system of people and processes that comprise your public key infrastructure.

The secure server that digitally signs the certificates is now called your certificate authority (CA). It can also revoke certificates if they are compromised, reach the end of the time you have determined they should exist or any other reason you wish to revoke them. The certificates themselves are the digital signatures which usually contain the user's (can be a computer program or object) name, public key and other data. The server that interfaces with the users, usually by presenting a form to collect information from the user, is called an registration authority (RA). It submits this information to the CA. PKI systems are still very complicated and vendor specific. You will almost surely need extensive vendor support or consultant.

Bots

Need constant information from the web but don't have time to spend searching every day? The answer may be bots, or web robots. A search bot can troll search engines and web sites, recording instances of words or prices. A tracking bot, on the other hand, can constantly access a specific link, returning a constantly changing data point, such as a stock index, or environmental recordings like humidity.

This is especially useful for developing statistics and large data banks about your own company's sales, and the demographics of potential customers.

Bots can do a great deal more than search the web. There are knowledge management agents, news agents, chatterbots, and several others kinds of bots. Many are free. The best web site to see what is going on with bots is *http://www.botknowledge.com/*. This site reviews all of the bots and leads you to the bot site when you are ready. Here are a few useful sites:

http://info.intelliseek.com/prod/bullseye.htm

Bullseye2 performs automatic searches. It can be scheduled and it e-mails you the results.

http://informant.dartmouth.edu/

The Informant also performs searches for key information and e-mails you a notification when it gets results.

http://www.endnote.com/

EndNote queries online reference databases, adds references to papers, and puts things into approved formats.

http://www.company.sleuth.com/index.cfm

Company Sleuth gathers voluminous information about any listed company, summarizes the information, and presents it in readable form.

http://www.worldfree.net/

KnowAll provides answers in plain text to natural language questions.

http://www.alexa.com/

Alexa learns about what you like best and suggests sites. It provides statistics about sites.

http://www.enfish.com/index.asp

Enfish Tracker Pro organizes information automatically and sets up folders for text information.

http://www.megaputer.com/

Text Analyst is a program that examines a text file and creates a semantic network of importance. It automatically produces an abstract.

http://www.spyonit.com/Home

SpyonIt creates "spies" that report back to you on almost any topic. Here is the review from botknowledge:

> SpyonIt's free service will change the way you use the Internet. SpyonIt uses bots to surf the web for you and notify you of information that you request. SpyonIt allows you to "program" spies to keep an eye out for certain information for you. Don't let the word "program" scare you. Telling the spies what to look for is easier than getting your email. Instead of wasting time looking and surfing through the millions of web pages, these spies will do the legwork for you. You can have an army of spies in the trenches while you increase your productivity and use your time reading, not searching.

One warning—make sure your data is critical and not readily available from another source. Making a bot is not only expensive, but also is very interesting. This leaves ample room for over-coding, and bot features that aren't answers to critical path issues, but instead answer queries made up during the coding process, and not at all necessary but merely novel data. Bot projects can get expensive in a hurry.

Browsers and mail servers

Although Netscape is still popular with a huge number of users (especially in Educational and medical institutions) at this point, it is difficult to recommend it as a long-term strategic path. Not only has Explorer jumped ahead of Netscape in general use, but since Netscape has been acquired by AOL, Netscape's quality has suffered as well. It's little wonder too, as AOL is running a brisk Internet conglomerate using it's own proprietary system. So lately the more popular browser questions have been about transferring out of Netscape Messenger, and how necessary is it to keep web pages first and foremost Netscape readable? Your web masters are guiltily rejoicing, because in the next three years, the daunting task of recreating two sets of code for each page will be unnecessary except in rare instances.

Switching from Netscape Messenger mail server application to Outlook (or Outlook Express) mostly involves exporting address books and very important mail. There are several available export formats to chose from, but the two most popular are .ldif and .csv. .ldif is a better export format than .csv (Comma Separated) for address books because the data fields don't match up to Outlook's Standard. On the other hand, .csv will probably catch up and pass the .ldif format over the next few years because it's so parsable for Eudora, online address books like Yahoo, and even Excel spreadsheets.

Try simply forwarding critical (hopefully less than 50) pieces of mail to the new Outlook Explorer application. Direct translation from the Netscape mail format to Outlook mail format is very difficult for someone who is not intimate with mail file and directory systems. Mail files are very difficult for the non-technical user to move from directory to directory without losing data. Don't try it unless you know what you are doing.

There are difficulties with archiving text in a mail format as well, because it is very difficult to export, move, and keep track of outside the specific user's mail application. One way is to keep all mail in the MS Word standard .doc. Archiving in the .doc format has plusses and minuses however. .doc plusses are that they are generally easy to move around a directory structure, and are readable on most platforms. The minuses are large file sizes, and .docs do not have a standardized format from year to year, leaving artifacts even between W98 and W2k documents.

Outlook mail format archiving minuses include: poor standardization and major security issues. Outlook is a very common target for virus makers, and is rather weak on security anyway. On the other hand, if you have the resources available to hire a mail expert—the inevitability of mail—it's ease of editing and familiarity make email archiving very pleasant and essentially inevitable. In other words, you already have a mail archive; you just didn't see it that way. Where are your important, but old, emails right now? As often as not, one large folder named "important data," or "Contacts and records I can't lose." A giant directory that should be cleaned and gone through but isn't. And once it's archived, that's usually the practical end of accessibility, unless it's one directory away and saved with a useful subject name. Build a directory system now and use it.

In-house small-scale reference and instructional documentation

One excellent, and simple, way to keep documents well referenced is to keep them as a .doc on a proxy server with hyperlinks to pertinent information. Save it as an .html document, and insert links "hyperlinks." To any Office document. It works as a very simple reference online text for users. Setting it up as a shortcut on desktops can function as a growing instruction manual or database map, as points in a document are just as simple to insert as whole pages.

Web development

Explorer 5.x has a nearly perfect support for CSS (Cascading Style sheets), which should cut hours out of .html production time, though Dreamweaver 3.x users have been able to create universal changes with application based tools for a while. Cascading style sheets are a protocol where variables are used instead of a value (such as color, or font size) or even a link. When a change is needed for the page, a single change in the "Head" of a Web document will make changes throughout an entire site.

Essentially all image manipulation has fallen into the hands of Photoshop, and Imageready (Adobe, bundled with Photoshop) is a simple and efficient export application, turning .psds into .jpeg and .gifs. The universality of .jpeg and .gif has made an excellent doorway between the Macintosh designers, and the PC page development teams. Mac is still holding a firm grip on the design community, so be prepared to accept images in Mac format, or request .gif or .jpg as attached documents if possible.

Most web page production has been split into two parts, with first-tier Dreamweaver page makers for layout and text insertion, while troubleshooting is handled by someone else who understands html and JavaScript. This also ends up being where links are maintained, though simple training can put this back in the hands of the Dreamweaver users, freeing the coder's time for more complex tasks.

Appendix A
How to Find and Retain Good IS People

Achieving World-Class Results Requires World-Class People

You do not need an entire staff of world-class employees to achieve success, but you certainly do need some. The achievement capability level of your best people determines your theoretical upper limit of success. Realistically, however, you will likely achieve far less than that theoretical level.

Do not be mislead by the fact that a well-organized and motivated group of level-B people will easily outperform a disorganized and unmotivated group of level-A people. Just remember that a well-organized and motivated group of level A people will outperform a well-organized and motivated group of level B people.

All of this is intended to encourage you to put your most intense and concentrated efforts into getting world-class people to work for you. You want to find people who are better than you. You may have become an IS manager because you have consistently been highly skilled. But to build on that, you must attract (and keep) IS people who are better than you are. You want to attract and keep IS people who are better than anybody.

As an IS manager, or any manager for that matter, you often do not have total control over such issues as salary. The corporation will dictate a specific budget to you, and you must work within those parameters. However, there are other non-advertised ways to get extra money for salary offers in your organization. There are some very savvy, not to say crafty, people in the organization who know these secrets. They may or may not be in human resources but you have to identify them, get them to like you or at least respect you, and then very patiently wait until they decide to help you on special occasions. Money is limited—use it wisely. Special favors are limited—use them wisely.

So how do you find these world-class people? Advertise. Talk to the marketing people. They know the principles, they know the level of effort required, and they know how to compare the cost of advertising to the return on investment. You must figure out what it is worth, in advertising dollars, to get a higher-level LAN administrator, programmer, or web designer.

Talk to the IS people working for you and see if they know anyone who highly skilled, shares the vision of the corporation and the department, and might be interested in a challenging job. If you can create a sense of excitement, challenge, and mutual care among your staff, they might be motivated to attract their friends and colleagues to your organization.

Mix consultants in with your employees. Consulting firms are good at attracting talented IS people who are experienced and often fairly good teachers as well. It is important that you make it clear that you will only accept very competent people. You should have no qualms whatsoever about rejecting people who do not hit the ground running and work well with your people. Keep your relationship with the consulting firm very friendly, but be ready to reject three or four consultants for every one you keep.

Interviewing the Technical Employee

If you have not had extensive interviewing experience, there are some basics you should know. For instance, you may be subconsciously influenced by how the prospective employee cuts their hair, how they are dressed, and how firmly they shake your hand when they look you in the eye. You may not be prepared for these responses, but you need to know how powerfully they may affect you. And you need to understand that physically appearance and bearing may have no reflection at all of a person's knowledge and capabilities.

You will also be influenced by how well prospective employees respond during the interview. People who answer your questions with one word might frustrate you, but IS people who can solve a complex problem with few words are invaluable. An applicant who is good at interviews will expand on answers with examples of their experience, and will tell you things about their approach to dealing with problems. It will be much easier and enjoyable to interview them. But the important thing to remember is that you are not so much hiring a person who is a good interviewee as much as a skilled computer technician. It doesn't hurt if they are good at interviews, but do not let communication skills lead you to select better interviewers over better employees.

Ask questions that lead the applicant to reveal what they know, what they have done, and who they are. Do not ask your mail administrator applicant, "Have you had much experience with Microsoft Outlook, or Group-Wise, etc.?" Instead, ask them, "How would you design a mail system that works well for the users and doesn't fail too often?" If experience in the specific mail system is very important to you, add a second question after they have answered the first question such as, "How would that be done in Outlook/GroupWise etc.?"

Give more weight in your evaluations to strong character, self-initiative, good practices, and extensive general experience than to specific experience with the product you use. Specific experience is often very important, but it is easier to learn Oracle than to learn to be creative and dependable. Make that a distinguishing principle for close calls. Just do not get too carried away with your opinion of how good you are at predicting character from an interview.

Once you sense that the person you are interviewing is the person you need for the job, roles will immediately switch. You become the applicant and they become the interviewer. Recognize that moment and give your prospective new employee a sense of your vision for what the organization can accomplish and how they will become a key part of that vision. If you know how to give employees responsibility and interesting challenges, tell them how you will do that. The most important thing you can do to attract world-class people is to give them a sense of the vision and importance they will be part of when they join your organization.

Retaining Skilled Employees

You keep employees by paying them roughly the going market rate and by providing a good place to work. Be on the alert for frustration indicators such as too much stress in some people and boredom in others. People who are bored in their work perform poorly and often spend time dreaming about another job. Fortunately, the information technology field provides tremendous opportunities to avoid boredom. Just do not get lax in your job as a manager and fail to see when people are getting trapped in repetitive work.

If you follow the management principles listed here you will give people a lot of independence and responsibility. You will avoid telling them what to do. Instead, tell them what needs to be accomplished and let them figure out what needs to be done to accomplish the goals.

Everyone seems to agree that IS people love to learn new things. A lot of that is achieved by being aggressive in your adoption of new technologies. I recognize the benefits of being slightly behind the early adopters of new technologies. Just be aware that if you consistently lag too far behind new technologies, the really creative and effective people will begin to drift off into jobs with other companies. You do not have to entertain them by letting them play with every new toy that comes along, but you absolutely have to challenge the technical abilities of your best people. The best people are usually four or five times more efficient and effective than the second best people. Do not let them get bored.

Training is an extremely difficult problem. The money is tough of course; almost all good courses are expensive. Computer-based training is becoming more effective but is still also expensive and will always be six months to a year behind good classroom training. Aside from the money though, it is very, very difficult to find time to send the best people to training. It is far easier to send the less critical people to class so they get most of the training. Of course, they need the training to improve, but your best people will return much more return on your investment dollar. Creative people will become more valuable to you through their interface with other people in training classes. They love to learn. That is how they got as good as they are. It can hurt your current project to let your stars go to training, and you may be criticized—but do it anyway.

Flexibility is key to keeping your employees happy. Be very, very flexible about letting people take care of their families. Make them feel comfortable about taking time off with no prior notification. People have jobs because they want to take care of their families. Set an example of diligence and hard work. Work plenty of long hours yourself. That way they know the flexibility for their family is out of concern for them and that the usual way is dedication and hard work. Do not give them the impression that it is unimportant that they take time for sick children or that their family concerns are low priority.

In Conclusion

People love to succeed in important tasks, they love to be challenged, they love to get paid, and they appreciate concern for their families and personal needs. Give your people all the independence and responsibility you can offer. Then work on how to get braver so you can give them more. If they fail, it is natural to feel disappointed. Let them know you are disappointed in the results but that you trust them. Then figure out together how they will succeed next time. Then really shock them by giving them even more responsibility in the same area.

Appendix B
Implementing an Internet Project

How to Deploy Web Technology in an Organization

It is likely that you have already started implementation of web technology in your organization. You may have a web site and are now thinking seriously of what e-commerce might mean for your company. Following are some suggestions for how to take that technology to the next level.

There are stages that most organizations must go through to integrate web technology into the culture of the organization. These are not just stages that the IS department has to go through—they are just the catalysts, the initial providers of infrastructure. Understanding the tools and the ways in which they might be used to benefit the core mission is a must for the rest of the company as well.

The first step in changing the way you do business using web technology is the part you have probably already begun—getting people familiar with the Internet. You probably have an Internet site already, but is the care and feeding of the Internet solely an IS responsibility or is has it moved into the corporate culture?

The best way to move Internet technology into the corporate culture is to ensure that the business people (i.e., non-IS staff) understand and use it. In addition, the business people should also be the content providers to the web site. Read that again and believe it—do not allow your IS people to put the content onto the web site. The site may be designed by the IS staff, but once it is in place the business people must have the tools enabling them to put content directly on the web site.

At the inception of a new corporate web site, IS staff members must introduce web concepts and tools to the rest of the organization. Some departments of the organization will likely have staff members who are already experts in web technology. This knowledge should be encouraged. Allow them to expand this knowledge as quickly as they can. Then the IS staff can instruct the rest of the staff who may be afraid of technology or who are slow in adopting it. The IS department often wants to maintain standards and take ownership of the web. It is important to have good tools and consistent rules in place, however they may need to be sacrificed for speed and breadth of adoption by non-IS people in the early stages. This is a race where the fastest will win, and the most organized will only get honorable mention.

Although your IS staff will prefer powerful and more complex web tools, business people should be given simple tools that they can be successful with quickly. When they outgrow the simple tools, you can provide them with something more advanced. The IS staff should not be a bottleneck preventing a business person from putting useful information directly onto the web site—and the reverse is true as well. When the IS staff trains groups in how to put information on the web, those groups will want their newly trained web people to take information from everyone else in the company and put it on the site themselves. This should also not be allowed to happen.

The way to transform an organization and move forward on the Internet is by having the first responsible source of information put the information directly on to the web. Any approval processes should be discouraged. Staff members should be responsible for both the accuracy and the speed of posting. This cab be a very difficult cultural transition. Most corporate systems are designed to avoid mistakes, and therefore typically contain slow approval processes. If mistakes are made in putting information on the web, it is better to find out why and fix the process rather than slowing down all the other processes that are not introducing mistakes.

The key to the system is to clearly identify the person actually putting information on the particular page. There should not be an organization, nor a committee, nor an office symbol listed as the content provider—just a real human being with a name, an e-mail address, and a phone number. This provider should be the person who is the most reliable source for the information. Instant feedback is the most effective teacher, creating a one-to-one correspondence between data and provider—instantly adjustable information provided by an instantly accessible author. This is the magic of the Internet.

Introducing an Intranet Site

An Internet site is generally regarded as a source of information for people outside of an organization. After your organization understands the care and feeding of an Internet site, it is time to introduce the intranet site. An intranet site is a site for internal use designed to improve the flow of information within an organization. Because actual work will be accomplished on this site, it will probably house complex applications.

The intranet site will also house information designed to be seen by insiders only. Security becomes very important here. The security on an Internet site is designed to prevent unauthorized changes. Security on an intranet site is needed to guard against bogus input as well as unauthorized viewing. After both an Internet and an Intranet site has been established, it is imperative to make it clear to your organization exactly which information is appropriate for each site. That distinction will become extremely critical when you move to the third stage—the extranet.

Your first Internet site was probably just bare advertising. Your first Intranet site will probably be the web version of a bulletin board. People will begin posting all sorts of notices and updates. After a short time people may no longer look at the sites because they are not updated regularly or they contain useless information. Usage can be measured by putting a web counter on every relevant page. When pages are no longer used, make that information widely known and understood. Force people to rethink the information that goes on the intranet and to improve the value of what is put up there.

Sooner or later, to improve the value of the information, more complex web applications will have to be provided. The vast majority of the information will not come from people typing information onto the web page. The information will be automatically updated in real-time by a wide variety of databases and other automated sources. Think about creating a system in which someone can highlight a portion of an e-mail and drag it directly onto the web site. E-mail is often the first source of new information within an organization. Make the transfer of that information to the web fast, accurate, and easy.

Here is a hint for how to introduce new technology across an organization: teach the administrative assistants first. Administrative assistants are often quick learners and usually have a good sense of the usefulness of new communications tools. They also understand the organization and its needs in a broader sense than many other people because of their daily contacts. When people complain about how hard the new technology is to learn, tell them who is already using it. Tell them to ask the administrative assistants for help, they have been using it for a while.

Taking It a Step Further—Extranets

After a while you will have developed a broad system of useful tools and information on your intranet. Some of this information would be extremely helpful to people outside of your organization. The resource used to provide outsiders access to your intranet is called an extranet. The potential for increased efficiency is enormous, however, the potential for security problems is also enormous.

How can you provide some of the information to outsiders without compromising the security of your internal site? The answer is your directory. A powerful and well-tested directory will allow you to very precisely control access to information on your intranet. You can control by name or group exactly who can access information on your Intranet and precisely which bits of information they can see.

For example, Company A might be able to view your entire hardware inventory by week over the last three years. Maybe they are your hardware supplier and you want them to anticipate when you need a new shipment and prepare for it rather than waiting for you to ask. Company B might be able to view your plans for a new office layout. You can control by company, by group and by individual exactly who can see, or modify, any information on your site.

Once the employees in your company understand this and get good at it, they will be able to invent entirely new ways of doing their jobs. The potential for increased efficiency and effectiveness in your company can explode. Show your IS people the vision of where you can go. Let them take over and get you there at Internet speeds. You must inform your boss of your plans so you can obtain financial resources and also explain the flurry of activity. With support from both senior management and staff alike, the sky is the limit in what you can accomplish.

Appendix C
Keeping Up with Your Newfound Internet Responsibilities

So, you've been transferred to head of IS or suddenly your umbrella has been extended into looking over the Web folks down the hall. And you're a hard worker, a quick study, and a good manager. Honestly though, you aren't a geek, and you're faking your way through the technology parts. This happens all the time because there's a desperate need for technology workers who are good managers, but often one half of the equation is missing. Your job is to become "Wired" by Monday. Well the good news is that nobody is ever truly "caught-up" in the Internet universe, because the technology moves faster than humanly comprehensible. The real job is to be able to constantly learn, constantly expand, and constantly play catch-up. The cliché of "surfing" waves of information is an apt one.

The upside is that you can't get too far behind either, because data that's two years old is simply compost for the endlessly rising data pile. The skills required include sniffing out new ideas, stepping back to look at emerging trends, and being able to abstract complex information into clear and simple statements. These are the manager's technology requirements.

Getting Up to Speed—Great Sources

Over and over the best IS managers cite periodicals, magazines, and technology news sites as their sources for information. This works against the grain of corporate culture, however, because people who are sitting around reading are not considered to be "working." It probably means lots of magazine perusal after work and on weekends, but don't pretend that a half-hour at lunchtime is enough to keep in the flow of things. It's going to be a couple of hours a day for a while before you discover the magazines that are pertinent to you. Just go to a big bookstore and hit the computing section of the periodicals rack. Start browsing and don't stop until the place closes. Don't bother with the book section either—that's for focused reading when you know what you need precisely. The magazines are more like an environment to graze in, don't worry about any one bite, because what you want is a little taste of everything.

When you pick up a copy of *BYTE Magazine,* you're probably going to be rather daunted by the sheer volume of incomprehensible articles. It will stay that way for a while, but just remember that it's that way for everyone. Start skimming articles that pertain to your important subjects today. You need a new server? Go look at the hardware and RAID Array articles. Skim the margin boxes on Apache and Linux. You won't understand most of what you read; accept it and get used to it. Skip to another subject that interests you. Learn to skim.

Is Dreamweaver still king? What's the status of Mozilla? What *is* Mozilla? You'll start with almost no understanding of any subjects, but soon there will be cross-references. Pick up *Web Developer Magazine* and browse Java articles for information on the latest tools. You're not a Java coder, so just read articles that discuss client relations, or emerging ideas, or perhaps good interfaces. Don't plough too deeply into stuff you don't understand, just keep moving. Remember, there's lots of paper on that rack. Buy 10 different magazines, and remember to write it all off as a tax deduction. Expense it even, whatever you can get away with. Subscribe to those magazines, because if you don't you'll let the whole thing slip. Magazines should become a constant background buzz at your fingertips. Some people keep old issues, but they don't seem to go back to them, and old copy certainly isn't part of "media as current environment."

There is a general set of technology news sources that will prove to be an excellent starting point for you to gather technology information. For the most general information on a daily basis, try these sites:

http://www.sjmercurynews.com/svtech/
http://www.zdnet.com/anchordesk/

To pull even further back, turn to either:

http://www.fortune.com/fortune/

or

http://www.wired.com

It should come as no surprise that *Fortune* magazine has turned hard and fast into a new economy-focused magazine and website. Meanwhile, *Wired* magazine has moved into the mainstream to keep its place as the culture's "Hip technology source" standard bearer, though *Wired* is more focused on technology culture than technology itself. For meatier daily news, and arguably the most referred to news source by the technically literate, check out www.slashdot.org for everything "Geek" on the planet today. Slashdot is the most savvy of the news sites lately, and because of its popularity with system administrators around the world, Slashdot often has inside scoops direct from the source. Sources that may even circumvent the public relations department. You usually hear it at Slashdot first, whether it's the Microsoft court case, Nanotech developments, or a leak of the latest Apple machine spec.

http://www.zdnet.com/eweek/, on the other hand, will provide a more focused stream of Internet information, and the there's lots of community resources there to answer the seemingly unanswerable. If you want a great source of information on networking as a whole, check out http://nwfusion.experts-exchange.com/. If you need to keep up with Apple news, http://macworld.zdnet.com/ and the evangelical http://www.macaddict.com/ will prove excellent sources for OS X information. And Mac Addict always has the best articles on why Macintosh "should" take over the world, and a host of accompanying commentary explaining Bill Gates' nefarious plans to keep Apple down.

Making the Most of the Internet

There are two general purposes to the Internet, one of which I'll get to later in this appendix. The first goal is to provide pertinent information as fast as possible to the user. It isn't often met, and the hurdles will make you just want to dial 411, ask your secretary, call your mom, or go find a dictionary—anything to avoid using the Internet. It is a valid complaint. However, there are some general tool sites out there that will often ease and expedite the task at hand if you are willing to put in a little practice. The following sections are ones that I use on a day-to-day basis for any of a number of reasons. They are certainly personal preferences rather than a set of rigid endorsements.

For searches I have two main sites. When I know what I'm looking for, I go to http://www.google.com/. Google searches the widest spectrum of the Web and has a very clean interface. http://hotbot.lycos.com/ is where I go when I don't know what I'm looking for, because Hotbot provides an array of subject headings and fields that will herd me into some niche of the Internet I never knew existed. This is pretty handy sometimes. If you want to know the search systems of tomorrow, go to http://bots.internet.com/ and see what's going on with Bots. This site is filled with the latest and greatest on Bots. And although they haven't taken over the Internet today, wouldn't it be nice to be at least partially aware of a technology on the horizon? I use http://www.dictionary.com/ to find words, http://www.mapquest.com/ to find places, and http://www.smartpages.com/ to find people and businesses. I still keep a dictionary and a phone book handy though—paper has its advantages.

When I want to buy a product online I start at http://www.mysimon.com/, which has the nifty feature of trolling the Web for all instances of a product and listing them according to price (or several other criteria) with a vendor who is given a reliability rating. This, in turn, has usually led me to either http://www.onvia.com for its wide range of products, or http://www.outpost.com for great prices and fast delivery. Outpost.com also has the funniest commercials I've ever seen.

Before you buy anything, though, it is critical to review endlessly. The systems administrators will have opinions, so will the web page designers, the secretaries, and so on. And if it pertains to their field, and you are a good manager, you will listen to them. You should also look on http://www.zdnet.com/, and http://www.zdnet.com/pcmag/ to see what the critics think. Ziff Davis owns most of the technology magazines both on and offline, and their database of product reviews are gargantuan. Product reviews are actually an excellent starting spot to learn about any technology subject from a manager's standpoint. What you need to know is not how to keep a server running, but what sorts of problems arise during the task. Is it a hardware, software, or user issue? When will there be problems because of high volume? What other tools are required? These are the issues getting tossed around by the techs, and you will at least be able to listen without a slack jaw if you have heard of the tools they use.

Site Building

If you've never coded or built a Website, here is a project that will change your entire understanding of the Internet and how it really works and is used. This is the second goal of the Internet, which I referred to earlier. That goal is to allow an individual to change the Internet environment, to change the way it responds to you, and to change what the Internet is. You are going to build a website. It will take about six hours for the complete newbie.

To get into the swing of things head over to http://hotwired.lycos.com/ and check up on the latest Digerati news and art. Although they certainly are rather full of themselves, Hotwired manages to be an entertaining source for the general fads, movements, and attitude of the web development community. When you need breaks, go back to Hotwired and download fun cartoons. Get a pad and paper and make a very simple layout with two pages, one picture that separates a title and a paragraph of text. Then put in two links at the bottom. Make one of the links go to your second page and make the other go to a site you like. My first link was to *The New York Times.* Don't even worry about centering yet, just let it all fall along the left margin. Your second page can be more of the same, or maybe put in two pictures, one of which is a link itself. Remember to put in a link back to your first page.

Next, go to http://angelfire.lycos.com/ where you can build a personal Website for free without having any pop-up ads or intrusive code stuck onto your new site. Just sign up and start. The tutorials are excellent, and the available tools are not at all shabby for the price, which is free. http://hotwired.lycos.com/webmonkey/ also has excellent tutorials for the uninitiated. You could even snag an excellent shareware HTML editor at http://www.ultraedit.com. On the other hand, you could write all your code in Notepad, which will impress anybody who doesn't know anything about coding. Another thing you might want to get is a File Transfer Protocol (FTP) program in order to put your pages up on a server. You could just use Angelfire's "in browser" FTP Utility, but going to find your own is a good exercise. Try CuteFTP or LeechFTP or whatever else you find. There are lots of tools and utilities out there that basically do the exact same thing.

Start with just any old pictures and text, and remember that nobody will ever see it but you. It won't be half as ugly as my first site, let me assure you. Your real task here will be to grab images and snippets from around the Web, and put in links to any site that strike you. To fancy things up, go to http://hotwired.lycos.com/webmonkey/ for bits of code and more advice on how to set up a page. Web monkey's "How-to Library" is an excellent place to find all things Web related, from marketing to code to Web tool listings. The ultimate source for site building is http://www.w3.org/. The Web Consortium establishes "The Standard" for all Web code. Is your document well formed? Is that HTML readable by Explorer 5.0? www.W3C.org knows.

The real trick to this project is learning how to gather information and tools on the Web and then putting them to use. The process is one that will not only help you get stuff done, it will help you understand what your team is doing when they work, and it will help you understand what clients are tripped up by when they are trying to glean information from your own site. You will develop preferences and habits as you begin to do things to the Web, instead of just being a passive observer. We intuitively know how to click links, scroll around, and browse. That's all just like watching TV of flipping through a newspaper. It is harder to do things to a monitor, because we never did things to our televisions besides change the channel. Remember that it is only mindset and practice that holds you back though; it really isn't about brainpower when you're working on this level. Once you have turned the Internet into a two-way street, you will start to change the way you organize information. You will think in terms of users and team members with their own pages, and you will look at those pages as flexible, dynamic, sources of information.

Further Reference

For further reference, the following sites are referenced in this appendix:

    http://hotwired.lycos.com/
    http://hotwired.lycos.com/webmonkey/
    http://angelfire.lycos.com/

http://www.w3.org/
http://nwfusion.experts-exchange.com/
http://www.zdnet.com/anchordesk/
http://www.slashdot.org
http://www.wired.com
http://www.fortune.com/fortune/
http://www.sjmercurynews.com/svtech/
http://www.zdnet.com/eweek/
http://macworld.zdnet.com/
http://www.macaddict.com/
http://www.google.com/
http://hotbot.lycos.com/
http://www.outpost.com
http://www.onvia.com
http://www.dictionary.com/
http://www.fatbrain.com/
http://www.smartpages.com/
http://www.zdnet.com/
http://bots.internet.com/

Index